How to Manage a Retail Shoe Store.

A SERIES OF ESSAYS

BY

PROMINENT RETAIL DEALERS

PUBLISHED ORIGINALLY IN

The Boot and Shoe Recorder,

BOSTON, MASS.,

In Response to Prizes offered for Best Essay.

A Compendium of Valuable Information on the Subject.

BOSTON, MASS.,
BOOT AND SHOE RECORDER PRINT,
1888.

PREFACE.

THE essays given in this volume were originally published in the BOOT AND SHOE RECORDER, of Boston, Mass., in response to offers of prizes for best essays on the subject. The publishers of the BOOT AND SHOE RECORDER, desiring to bring out practical information on the subject, as well as to develop latent literary talent among the dealers, offered three cash prizes for best three essays in order of merit, on the subject of "How to Manage a Retail Boot and Shoe Store." In response to this offer, the articles were published in the BOOT AND SHOE RECORDER, in the order in which they appear in this volume. With the publication of the first nineteen articles, the first contest was closed, and the names of the writers were submitted to the subscribers of the RECORDER for a vote to award the prizes. The result of this vote was that the first prize was awarded to Mr. CHARLES DONEY, of Ottawa, Canada; the second prize to Mr. I. B. ARNOLD, of Champaign, Ill.; and the third prize to Mrs. RUTH BOND, of Brilliant, O.

In view of the fact that a number of other dealers wished to contribute essays on the subject, a supplementary contest was arranged for, and three additional prizes were offered for the best three essays in order of merit, on the same subject. These essays, twelve in number were published in the RECORDER, in the order as given in this volume, and the claims of the contestants for the prizes were again submitted to a vote of the subscribers of the RECORDER. The result of this vote was the award of the first prize to "OLD CALFSKIN," (G. M. FINK) Salem, O.; the second prize to "HIC JACET," New York; and the third prize to M. E. KREIDLER, South Bethlehem, Pa.

The essays embodied so much excellent and practical information on the subject, that there was a general demand for the republication in convenient form for reference, and to meet this demand, the present volume is published. Any commendation of the merit of the essays would be superfluous, as they show for themselves, and represent the best thoughts and experiences of the best minds in the retail shoe trade.

How to Manage a Retail Shoe Store.

BY CHARLES DONEY, OTTAWA, CAN.

In writing upon a subject of this kind for publication in a journal having such a wide and extensive circulation as the BOOT AND SHOE RECORDER, one sees numerous difficulties which have to be in part overcome before any such article can become of interest to readers whose locations are from California to the northermost part of Canada and away beyond the seas to wherever the Anglo-Saxon and his tongue are found. Among such a vast number of mercantile men living and doing business under many very different conditions and requirements, it is, to say the least, an arduous task to set before a man who simply professes to buy and sell shoes, to write of the general principles which ought to govern the management of a shoe store in all of those many climes, latitudes, people, and varied ideas which find place within the great Anglo-Saxon race. However, you or your subscribers will not ask for perfection, but merely that a discussion shall be caused, and the BOOT AND SHOE RECORDER be enabled thereby to prosecute its good work of conveying, spreading and sowing the best ideas having existence within the

shoe fraternity to the advantage and general advance-
ment of that great industry.

As a first proposition, in starting, the owner of a
shoe store should build all his plans upon one great
principle, viz., his store is for the convenience and
general accommodation of an ever-exacting public,
and he simply the warehouse-man in charge of a stock
from which the public will draw as their wants arise
and their means will afford them, the legitimate
profit arising from each transaction being the contribution of each purchaser toward the payment for his
services and their necessary expenditure to the management of the warehouse for the general good. Let
this principle be thoroughly grounded in the mind of
the head of a retail store, and then he will, as a natural result, seek all means possible to make his store
the chosen of the people.

Again I shall advance the argument, that the owner
of a retail store should consider himself a public man,
and within his sphere as much the property of the
people of his shoe constituency as the politician, who
also glories in thinking himself owned by the voting
power of his political constituency. The shoeman's
voters are the feet of the people, and he who can so
manage his stock as to make it agreeable to the
greater number of feet as they exist, and his store a
place which will welcome and make happy the minds
of the same majority who govern and control those
feet, will be the shoeman who at the polls of the
yearly balance sheet will find himself a long way
ahead.

We shall, therefore, base the arguments of this essay upon those general principles, and will commence operations by opening a new shoe store.

A new shoe store is a candidate for public favor. The public will ask that the store be as convenient to them as possible, and they will demand that it shall be as attractive as a shoe store can well be. They labor incessantly to make their own homes airy, comfortable, and pleasing to the eye, which produces contentment to the mind, and they do not want to go into the city or down town and enter a gloomy, wretched old shoe store in order that their nostrils be stuffed with the nasty, disagreeable odors, and their senses shocked by accumulated filth and an utterly disarranged establishment. Therefore, in choosing your location, make choice of the very best for the class of trade you intend catering for, and then fit it up as acceptably as possible to the taste of those whom you hope to draw upon as patrons of the stock and store. If you are going to be a candidate for fine trade, let your store be situated among the dry-goods houses that are doing it, and have your store fitted up as handsomely and as attractively as theirs. Do not let yourself suppose that mirrors, gold or silver ornaments are too good for your shoe store, for they are not, but will become to you visible modes of impressing upon the public mind the excellence and superiority of your shoes. It is natural to suppose, when you see a man's table laden with gold and silver and all the other purchasable riches of the earth, that he is not only wealthy, but that he is a gentleman of

taste, refinement and culture, and so will an ever-dis-
criminating public make up its estimate of your stock
by the ideas displayed at the direction of the mind
and man who governs it. If they are pleasing, and
supply, through the magnifying power of the eye, a
sense of interest, and, shall we add, of delight, from
such a source will be gathered the shoeman's greatest harvest. The public mind will be to itself un-
suspectingly trained up to the belief that that store
and that man has the best and prettiest shoes in town.
And this impression will not necessarily be wrong,
for in the nature of things the human mind that finds
an agreeable occupancy in dwelling within an atmosphere of cleanliness and comparative brilliancy will
almost be sure to influence its possessor to choose,
purchase and offer for sale the choicest and most
handsome wares that the world's creative power has
yet produced.

Whilst this law, in our opinion, should govern the
man who seeks his patrons from among those who
have wealth and its accompaniments, a somewhat different idea should prevail where staple or cheap
goods are to be the candidates for public favor. A
cheap store should be located right among cheap
stores, and its main inducement should be good value,
but the proprietors of cheap stores too often indulge
in this belief to the destruction of all business principles. They disregard all systematic arrangement
of stock, of books, of profits, of prices, of cleanliness,
of civility, to that great and often fatal craze of selling
cheap.

It is too often laid down as a law that a cheap store does not require as much capital as the finer trade because of its quick turn-over and the great difference in value of similar quantities. Here we shall say that this law is a fallacy. To make a cheap store successful, goods must be purchased right, and at bottom figures. To do this year in and year out, a man must have ready cash, whereas the man of fine trade must buy seventy-five per cent of his goods from the best makers at established prices, and he can, as a rule, obtain reasonable credit and a like extension too, if required. But cheap lots of low-priced goods must almost invariably be paid for by Mr. Cash. Therefore, we say to the man who desires to lead in cheap goods, see that you have ample capital. See that you buy right down to rock bottom figures every time. See that you obtain a paying profit, whilst take care that you offer indisputable value. Then stick to your price, and the public will soon learn to trust you. See that your store is kept cheerful, clean, airy and bright, and that your clerks are civil, and carry with them an agreeable mode of addressing your constituents. No man values a little considerate treatment more than the poor man, and why should he not obtain it when he enters your store with an honest dollar for investment? See that your stock is kept in systematic order, and that every line has its proper place. Have every boot and its size entered in the clerk's check book when sold, and at stated hours let it be some one's duty to replace the goods sold from the stock-room, and report to the office the lines and sizes that are low. By doing this you will rarely have to lose sales for want of sizes. A cheap store should discard credit altogether. It ought to be never given.

One cheap store item more and then we will revisit the haunts of fine trade. The largest proportion of cheap stores keep their stock in a dirty, slovenly state. This is a desperate and an insane fault. Because a man is poor is no reason why he should be shown a dusty boot in place of a clean one. A fresh, new-looking boot will sell at all times for twenty-five to fifty cents more than a mouldy image of the antiquated ages, and a continual exhibit of dust and filth will form a crust of impressions in the public mind which will formulate itself into an immovable belief that your stock is old and shop-worn. Allow that idea to be once fairly established in the minds of your purchasing constituents and your stock has depreciated in value by at least fifteen per cent. Then see to it that your clerks utilize their every spare ten minutes in the dusting, refreshing and replacing of your stock.

We will again discuss the whats and shoulds of a fine shoe store. A man suitable to succeed in the fine shoe trade should be, if it is allowable or possible for a shoeman to be, a gentleman. To know what ladies or gentlemen really require to satisfy their tastes and supply them with the comfort and ease they at all times seek, demands that the man himself should, in some degree, feel as they do, and, therefore, be in sympathy with their wants. A man possessing low, rough, uncultivated instincts can no more feel and sympathize with a lady's needs and demands than a heathen can comprehend and appreciate the beauty and purity of the Christian religion. Therefore we say to the man who dreams of opening out in the fine shoe trade, the first thing you examine is yourself. If you are not the correct article, then get out and away, for the store conducted by you will most surely fail.

If satisfied that you are all O. K. yourself, the location of your store well chosen, the fittings and general make-up brilliant, then attend to the purchasing of your stock. Do not buy too largely. You have entered into the fashionable world, and of all fickles known to humanity you will discover fashion to be the greatest. Buy carefully and secure fashion. The goods will be of but little value to you if they are not the latest of late styles. Buy also from the best known and most reliable makers. Do not risk your orders with new makers until you have obtained a thorough and indisputable knowledge of your business and the immediate demands of your locality. Your stock procured, then seek for aids in the shape of clerks. Whatever you do, do not have a low grade clerk in your store. Have them to be, as far as clerks can be, ladies or gentlemen. See to it that they not only speak civilly, but that they do it gracefully and without effort. Do not permit a black, frowning, walking image of satan in your store, who will frighten the dickens out of your customers, for one moment. Make quite sure that they are not too proud or too lazy to button a boot, take one off, put one on, or attend to any other reasonable request that a lady or gentleman has a right to make, and take good care that they do not lie about your goods. In the course of ten years a lie will be found to be the most unprofitable of bad investments. Business men too often think it smart in a clerk to fool a customer, and thereby make the sale; but do they as often consider how many of their patrons, once fooled, are forever driven from their store? A man who trusts in another because of his own personal ignorance of the special qualities of a shoe, will never forgive or forget the creature who took so mean and paltry an advantage of him as to lie and deceive for the sake of the sale of a pair of shoes. Again, do not work your clerks too many hours. A clerk that is sleepy for want of rest is to your store a standing sign of "customers, get out." There should be a welcome at all times emanating from your clerks' faces which will convey to the purchaser the pleasing belief that he or she is conferring a favor upon the clerk and the establishment. If persons cannot select what they want from your shelves, do not show displeasure, but bid them adieu with as much gratitude as if they had purchased, and insist that your clerks do likewise. Those persons will then some day return and leave you their money for your goods.

In the keeping of stock it is all-important that your cartons should exhibit freshness and a variety in their colors, and be labeled with description, maker, cost and selling price plainly written upon them. When goods are replaced in the cartons, see to it that every shoe is buttoned, laced or tied. Nothing appears so bad as fine goods opening out to a customer as if a dozen or two people had incased their feet within them. Every carton should have its designated place, and permit no such a chance as clerks hunting for goods in the presence of a lady or gentleman. To a well-ordered mind such an exhibition of management would necessitate the loss of faith in your stock and store.

Never permit more than one pair of a size of a line to be on the sale shelf at one time. To do so is a certainty of your having shop-worn goods, for if several of a size remain together on the sale shelf, the result is that they are all tried on and off, and before they are all disposed of you have sluggards that are shorn of all their external and internal beauty, whereas with the one pair in any live store it cannot remain on the shelf long, and when sold will be replaced with a bran new, clean shoe from the stockroom. Keep a register of your sales, and every night write off to the makers for the sizes you are sold out of. In expensive, fashionable goods, you should never purchase heavily; therefore it is all-important that your stock should be systematically watched and renewed frequently. Fashion you should study continually, and watch her as if she were a great, huge thief, for it will startle you some fine morn to find how much of your hard-earned profits she has robbed you of, if you are not up to her and not forever after her. It is only by constant care that you can keep

astride with her ever-changing attitude, and see to it
that you have a good, straight profit on all fresh ar-
rivals of such goods, for in seventy per cent of purchases you will have to do some sacrificing before you
are through with them. In the law of systematic
profits we do not believe ; it is none of the public's
affairs what you pay for your goods. It is simply a
matter of how much value there is in that shoe, and
we say get out of that shoe all you in honesty can.
If a shoe has cost you a dollar, and it is only worth
fifty cents, the public will sneer at your talking a dollar to them. Then we say if it costs a dollar only
to you, and there is straight value to the public for
three, charge the public three for it, and you have
done what is just to your own self in buying so much
value for little money.

In the cash department never neglect having a
system as perfect as the means at your disposal will
furnish for checking all cash transactions. If there
is a leak there, all your other efforts, no matter how
brilliant, will fall into a nothingness, as the seed sown
on the sea-shore.

Do not demean your establishment by doing anything which can be termed small with your customers.
A shoeman should uphold the honor of his store to
the public with as much tenacity and minuteness as
the banker. There is money in training the people
to regard your store with implicit confidence. If a
person purchases at your store a shoe, and afterward
asks that his or her money be returned, and the shoe
is not injured, return it. Do not allow that person to

suppose for a moment that a single pair of shoes is of any consideration to you. Such an individual will long remember that action, and some day will get treated far differently elsewhere, and will then return to you and be one of those who will swear by you. The writer carries this plan out in his own store, and finds it one of his best investment plans.

In conclusion, have a thorough system for everything. Deal honestly with your shoe constituents, and do not ever forget that you owe the same duty to yourself. Never think of selling new goods unless you have a fair, and, every time you can, a good profit. Labor earnestly for the confidence and esteem of the public. Insist upon the exhibition of pleasing faces and a generous civility by your clerks to all and to whomsoever may enter your store. Show no compunction for any employe who disobeys or does not give proper heed to your rules, regulations and instructions. See that your store is clean and orderly, and that your stock is ready to be shown without a moment's delay. Pay special attention to your show window, and do not grudge labor or expense to make it an object of admiration. Do not be afraid to clear out old stock at whatever it will bring, but do not try that game with new. Be strictly accurate in your book accounts, and take stock at least once in every year. Go through your stock two or three times in each year, and mark down ten per cent of whatever is sticking on the shelves, and mark it down again and again until you bring it to a selling basis; but take good care that you never buy the same line again that called upon you for a mark down. Have your store opened punctually every morning at the customary hour, and never close it one minute before the recognized or established time at night. Have all promises made in the store by clerks, or otherwise, faithfully executed, even though loss may attach itself to the performance. In other words, never be caught playing with your shoe constituents. Light your store thoroughly. There is no such good advertisement as a well-kept, well-lit store. Never advertise what you have not got or what you do not intend to sell. Again we say do not fool or trifle with the publ'

How to Manage a Retail Shoe Store.

BY WIN S. WELD, ELGIN, ILL.

Neatness attracts ; slovenliness repels. Cleanliness of the floor, orderly arrangement of goods, cases, settees, are as possible where the appointments are simple and cheap as where the furnishings are ornate and costly. Let there be a carpet—rag, Wilton or velvet—but let it be clean ; cleanliness is appreciated by all ladies, and some men. Neatness shows pride in your business ; pride follows success ; success comes only to those who deserve it. By these three steps men reason out prosperity from the appearance of your prosperous surroundings ; and so the appearance of prosperity breeds prosperity, for men like to deal with a success.

Prompt greeting of every person entering the door, and courteous treatment of all, is the first rule of conduct, and this courteousness must proceed from the genuine good fellowship which recognizes with the poet that

> "The rank is but the guinea-stamp,
> The man's the gowd for a' that."

Once fall into the habit of deferring to the well-dressed, and of gruffly treating the common when only one is present, and you will find yourself doing

it when both are nigh. The result will be the loss
of the custom of the independent poor, who are
quickly chilled on seeing your partiality. Let your
good nature be genuine, and then it will be all-em-
bracing. Keep the good-will of everybody. ·Better
have the good-will of a dog than his ill-will !"
Every man has his influence.

It is almost unnecessary to say that a good assortment of reliable and seasonable, medium-priced goods
is absolutely essential to meet the requirements of
the trade today; and it should be had when the
season opens. Keeping stock clean and in good
order is a prime requisite; goods taken from a box,
where they have been tumbled, do not seem so choice
as when carefully taken from appreciative packings.
Let your actions speak louder than words in appre-
ciating your goods; besides, care in handling will
pay in saving their finish. Ladies are your best customers, and quickly notice all these refinements of
business.

The most perplexing feature of any business is
the matter of giving credit. Our firm, after being
bothered with it long enough, adopted the "cash
system," and the result has been satisfactory. Of
course we allow goods to be taken home on approval,
but it is with the express understanding that they
must be paid for when selection is made. We have
a memorandum book whose leaves are perforated
twice, for this purpose, so that the duplicate can be
torn out. The following is the form of memorandum.

Perforated.. ....

MEMORANDUM

OF

GOODS TAKEN ON APPROVAL.

By..

From WIN. S. WELD & CO.'S

CASH SHOE STORE.

The same to be paid for when selection is made.

No..... ....188...

....

MEMORANDUM.

[Here follows a duplicate of the above, with the request that the slip be returned.]

The first remains in the stub book until the second is returned by the customer, when both are destroyed, and the entry made in the cash book. It might be well to add that we have not for a moment regretted the change to a cash system, and see no probability of our returning to the "trust and bust" way.

No one will deny that judicious advertising is one of the most important matters pertaining to any business, and it requires thought and special study of each case to secure the best results. The experience of our firm has demonstrated to its satisfaction that much good can be done by advertising specialties, as we thus arouse a laudable curiosity, which brings in inquirers ; and, should the specialty fail to suit, it is more than likely that we can please the customer from our regular stock, but at any rate we have either made a new acquaintance or reminded an old one that we still live. Advertisements should be cautiously and conscientiously worded. How often does one see : "We carry the largest stock—the best assortment— at lowest prices in town." Will some such advertiser inform us how these claims can attract attention or inspire the confidence of the people? Such words, in our estimation, have absolutely no weight. We leave out all such claims, and speak fully of different articles, explain their merits. Then change advertisements often, so as to keep fresh ideas before the people, and above all make it a point to tell the truth in our advertisements, so that when special bargains are offered, the public may confidently know that there is really something in store for them. There are many schemes and ways of advertising, but no matter which or how many we use, a strict adherence to the truth is the only safe way. Honesty is the only good or best policy in advertising.

After an honest inquirer comes as a result of honest advertising, any attempt to influence him to buy what he does not want is a fatal error. While it may for the time being swell the cash account, yet the patron will forever blame the merchant for influencing him

against his own judgment, and will be almost sure to
retaliate by trying other dealers. It is from the steady
custom of the intelligent and liberal buyer that the
profitable business is built up. Every intelligent buyer
knows that no ordinary stock can meet his varied
wants on every occasion, and you will gain his confidence more frankly admitting (with regrets of course)
that this time you cannot supply him; and you will
make much more money to let him go than to sell
him what he really does not want. It is an easy matter to ascertain the nature of the service expected by
the buyer, and goods suitable to the occupation of the
wearer should always be offered first. If you cannot
suit, then dismiss him, always with a kind word for
some neighbor dealer who may have what he wants,
and always speak kindly of legitimate competitors.
The red-flag anarchists of the auction room do not
deserve consideration.

The question which this contribution seeks to answer,
has thus led up to a consideration of the aim one has
in embarking in the business, for much depends upon
the end aimed at; that is, whether the intention is
merely to make money, or whether added to and
coupled with this there be a desire of building up a
permanent reputation for business sagacity and character that would both be a satisfaction to the possessor
and also create a noble emulation in those around him.
In other words, one should have a desire to benefit
himself, and also to benefit the world by strengthen-
ing his own character, and thus by reflex to elevate
the character and influence the destiny of one's

fellows. This should be the aim in all business, but
special care should be taken in the shoe trade, since
in the latter frequent opportunities offer us frequent
temptations to deceive the unsuspecting (?) public.

To our mind the man who makes a success of any
business is he who puts character into it until he
has acquired that most valuable of all mercantile
"good-wills," namely, the confidence of the people.
To secure this the dealer must have conscience and
faith in his business, must represent goods just as he
believes them to be, and, if he has been deceived,
then he must haste to do all that is reasonable to
make amends. By this course he will merit and
receive the confidence of the people, so that he can
sell goods on his sole recommendation, thus enabling
him to promptly reap the harvest of the early sales of
each new specialty at its first prices, where other
dealers cannot dispose of them until slow trial has
proven their value. From these early sales at good
prices come good profits and the reputation for enterprise, and all from simple persistence in honesty of
dealing.

He who follows out these general directions will,
with attention to buying, hardly fail to make a success
of the shoe business in any location where it is
reasonable to suppose there is a field.

Let us recapitulate :

Prompt service, good manners, neatness of store
and stock, pride in the same, cash deal, good goods
at popular prices, persistent advertising by telling the
truth through newspapers of character, remembering

that a customer unsuited causes an inevitable loss, and from first to last, mixing character with your business, as Rubens "used brains" to mix his brilliant and lasting colors.

How to Manage a Retail Shoe Store.

BY CHARLES DONEY, OTTAWA, CAN.

In writing upon a subject of this kind for publication in a journal having such a wide and extensive circulation as the BOOT AND SHOE RECORDER, one sees numerous difficulties which have to be in part overcome before any such article can become of interest to readers whose locations are from California to the northermost part of Canada and away beyond the seas to wherever the Anglo-Saxon and his tongue are found. Among such a vast number of mercantile men living and doing business under many very different conditions and requirements, it is, to say the least, an arduous task to set before a man who simply professes to buy and sell shoes, to write of the general principles which ought to govern the management of a shoe store in all of those many climes, latitudes, people, and varied ideas which find place within the great Anglo-Saxon race. However, you or your subscribers will not ask for perfection, but merely that a discussion shall be caused, and the BOOT AND SHOE RECORDER be enabled thereby to prosecute its good work of conveying, spreading and sowing the best ideas having existence within the "better class of stores," as it is in one of those I have learned what I know of the trade ; therefore, I will speak as I see it, and hope to read in some future article how the business is conducted by some of my brothers who do not pretend to cater for "the best trade only." Some of my ideas may seem extravagant ; but it is not supposed they will be followed out by a dealer who cannot afford the cost or expense they require. Let me first begin on the exterior of the store.

The outside of the store should be as attractive as possible, the windows kept clean, the wood-work well painted, or if hard wood well varnished, the signs fresh and clean, and the general appearance denoting taste and cleanliness.

Of the interior there is much to say about every particular. I will, therefore, take up the different topics briefly.

The floor of your store should be either entirely carpeted or a hard wood well finished up, and mats, rugs or strips of tapestry carpet laid in front of the seats. Small hassocks for the clerk to kneel on while trying on shoes are very desirable, while an umbrella stand, cuspidores, etc., should not be forgotten in the way of furniture.

The seats should be easy settees, or, as I have often seen them, pretty camp chairs. A large table set in the center of the store for ladies to lay parcels on is a necessity, while the cashier's desk should be in the rear.

The shelving should be arranged so the stock could be kept in cartons, and in many cases I have known dealers who had a uniform carton made at their own expense, handsomely labeled, containing the name, size, width, style, selling and cost price of the goods.

The woodwork and furniture should all match. It may be made of cherry, mahogany, walnut, ash or even white wood finished up in its natural color or to represent any of the kinds I have named. Cherry has always been my ideal of a handsome effect.

The gas fixtures should be polished brass, kept bright and clean, and in the summer months covered with fancy tartan to keep them free from fly and other dirt.

Departments for the different kinds of goods you keep are necessary. Men's, boys', youths', ladies', misses', children's, infants' goods, and your findings, should all be kept in departments separate from each other, and not scattered all over the store. Dealers will find this a great convenience in waiting on their customers.

Fresco your ceilings. This can be done now, in all large cities, at a small expense compared to the cost of years gone by. I remember in 1870, when I first commenced in the business, that the cost of frescoing our store was about $200. Last year we had the same store frescoed on a more elaborate scale for $75.

Take great pains in the care of your windows; they should be cleaned at least once a week in winter, and twice in summer, the bottoms should be covered with a pretty garnet: canton flannel, velvet, etc., is the material. Brass and nickel fixtures should be tastily arranged. I consider them the best investment that any dealer can make. They pay for themselves three or four times every year. Like your gas fixtures, keep them clean. A good chamois will do it.

Be careful of the stock you show in your windows. Do not let it get exposed to the sun. It would not take long to ruin several hundred dollars' worth of goods.

In dressing your windows, discretion, as well as taste, is necessary. There are times when low shoes, fancy shoes, slippers, heavy shoes and all other grades and makes should be carefully shown up.

The above is my idea of a first-class shoe store. It covers the plan I have laid out and followed for many years. I will now take up a few other subjects of importance connected with the management of a store.

See that your clerks are gentlemanly. Make them use your customers courteously whether they buy or not. If you don't succeed in selling them today, you may some other time. If they are not used right, depend upon it, they will not forget it, and will refuse to visit you when you may have a chance to sell them. You must expect trials as well as triumphs : all is not gold that glitters. Your clerks are paid by you, and should be made to show respect to all who enter your store.

Sell all your goods at one price. When you say that a certain shoe shall be worth $3.00, don't mean $2.50 or $2.75, let it be $3.00. If you can afford to sell it for less, make it at that figure on the start. This, I consider one of the most important factors in doing business. It will, in the end, cause confidence and popularity to come to you.

If possible, do a cash business. This I have not done. We have had a very large credit trade, but it has been of such a character, that year in and year out we have not lost as many dollars as you have fingers on your hands, but as a rule it is the opposite. If you have a large capital, and know who your customers are, you may be able to succeed. Unless you have these requisites, take my advice and do your business on a cash basis.

Keep your stock in good condition, look after your styles and sizes, always have them on hand, and you will not lose a sale. I adopted a method some years ago that has proved very successful. It was what I called a "stock book." In it I entered every pair of shoes I had come into my store, with the style and size of each. When a pair was sold I marked it in the book. I could always tell just the condition my stock was in. Here is a sample leaf.

MADE BY SMITH & JONES.
QUALITY, LADIES' FRENCH KID.
STYLE, COMMON SENSE.
WIDTH, B.

SIZES No.	3 3	3½ 3	4 3	4½ 3	5 2	5¼ 2	6 2
	x	x			x	x	x
	x					x	

The first numbers are the sizes, and those under them denote the numbers of pairs of each size.

When I sold a pair of 3 1-2, I put a cross under that size, and the same with every other size. By this I could always know what to order.

Be careful about buying; do not take this or that lot of goods because they *look well*. The question is, *Can you sell them?* If your trade calls for certain lines, styles or make, it is good policy for you to always have them on hand. Never order a second lot of the same kind of goods that has been a drag on your hands. In the late summer, work off your light goods as closely as your business will allow you, and in the late winter do the same to your heavy goods. Place your orders for new supplies well in advance of the season. You must remember that an order for a line of shoes cannot be filled in a week or a month. You must remember that manufacturers do not carry a stock on hand. It would not be policy for you or for them to do so. Styles change, stock changes, and your trade is constantly wanting changes, so when you order there is always some particular way you want your goods made, and the manufacturer who makes them must have the time to get up what you want. A man with an established trade can, in nearly every case, tell about what his trade will require for the next or coming season.

Never misrepresent, or allow your clerks to, any article you may have for sale. There is nothing that will make your customers lose confidence in you or hurt you more in your business, than to sell them an article, and represent it as being so-and-so, and have it turn out the opposite. When you take $5.00, give as near as possible $5.00 worth. I have known cases where some dealers have taken customers who were not posted on quality or worth and charged them from one-quarter to one-third more for the goods than they were actually worth. They evidently thought themselves smart business men, and that such transactions would, in time, bring them wealth; but, mark my words for it, few such men ever succeed. The day of reckoning comes at last.

Keep your books plain, have them in such condition that you may know how you stand at a moment's notice; this is as easily done as to have your business all mixed up. Enter your sales and post your ledger daily, and watch carefully your bills as they come due. Pay your debts promptly, and you will be sure to always get the lowest prices offered you in a trade. There is no manufacturer or jobber but who is very careful to know who his best-paying customers are.

The foregoing has been a part of my experience. As I said at the outset, I did not expect to give a plan that could be followed by all your readers, but I think many of them can take some pointers from my experience.

How to Manage a Retail Shoe Store.

BY F. GRIFFITH, SUCCESSOR TO GEORGE E. ANGEL &
CO., GRAND HAVEN, MICH.

It will be hard work to lay down a set of rules to govern all classes of retail shoe stores. Yet it may be possible to put on paper something that will serve as a guide to the retail dealer, no matter what class of goods he may handle, or where he may be located.

In starting a boot and shoe store, the first thing to be taken into consideration is the class of trade you wish to reach, whether the better or the cheaper. Having decided on that, the next thing in order is the store and location. No matter what class of goods you decide on handling, it is very important that your store be so located that a great many people will be passing and repassing every day. The room need not be so very large, as a medium-sized one, well fitted and filled, looks better than a great barn of a room partially filled; but that is something each one can decide for himself.

We will suppose that you have decided to reach the better class of trade, and so will proceed to fit up the store, and buy the stock with that understanding. Put in your shelving so that there will be a ledge about three feet from the floors, wide enough to set the cartons on when showing the goods. As most all shoes now come in single pair cartons, counters are unnecessary, if the shelving is put up right; that is, with the above-mentioned projection. It will give room and depth beneath for a set of drawers which come handy for various purposes. The shelves should be spaced so that three pairs of ladies' shoes in single pair cartons will set one upon the other between them. Now fit up the balance of the room, floors, windows, etc., so that everything will be just as neat and tasty as possible. Money invested in floor covering, fancy rugs, mirrors, settees and window fixtures, will bring in big returns. People like nice things, and when they step into a store and see everything nice, clean and attractive, they at once come to the conclusion that the goods handled are of the best.

Now arrange to have your store well lighted ; nothing makes a store more attractive in the evening than plenty of light; never try to economize in this. Having got your store in shape to receive the stock, the next thing in order is to buy it, or probably it will be better to do so while the room is being got ready.

Buying boots and shoes is a difficult undertaking, especially to a new beginner, and it will be best not to buy very heavy until you have learned the demands of your trade.

For the best class of trade it will be necessary to buy largely from the manufacturers. Buy from as few houses as possible, and get the goods you want. Buy as few kinds or styles as possible, yet don't think.

because you happen to like a certain shoe, that your customers will all think the same. You must have a variety; but don't buy everything you see. Most manufacturers make firsts, seconds and thirds of their different styles of shoes. Say the agent is showing you a ladies' kid button shoe, made on the Spanish arch last, and says, "This is our best grade of curacoa kid, and is worth three dollars a pair. Here is another sample made on the same last as the above, only the stock isn't quite as fine, that I can sell you at two dollars and a half; we will guarantee the wearing qualities of either of them." Now you look the two samples over, and if you are not well acquainted with shoes you will see but little difference in them, and would quite naturally ask, if you hadn't been told, what makes the difference in the price. That is just the question your customers will ask, should you put them in stock, and it will keep you and your clerks busy explaining the difference. You will understand; but seventy-five per cent of your customers will fail to do so, as they can see little or no difference in them, and so the two will constantly conflict with each other.

Now, if you want these two grades, buy them on different lasts, and see that there is enough difference in the appearance of the two, that one can't possibly be mistaken for the other. I think it works better to have your different priced shoes made by different manufacturers as far as practicable, especially in kid goods, or have the stamp left off the cheaper lines; this applies to all kinds of shoes, gentlemen's as well

as ladies' and children's. Of course, in buying, you will
want different style lasts as well as different widths, as
one style or width will not suit or fit every one. In
marking your shoes make them even money. Say you
start your ladies' kid button at two dollars, mark the
next grade two dollars and a half, and the next three
dollars, and so on, having fifty cents difference in the
price ; in your ladies' low cut goods twenty-five cents
difference may be enough ; but of course each one
can use his own judgment as to that. If you start
your gentlmen's shoes at two dollars make the next
price two dollars and a half, then three dollars. I do
not find it necessary to have a three-dollar-and-a-half
grade in gentlemen's shoes unless it is. in low-cut
goods, as I can buy a gentlemen's first-class, reliable
shoe to retail at three dollars, and make a good profit ;
by keeping a good assortment, you can supply your
trade that want a medium-priced shoe, and a three-
dollar-and-a-half grade would show so little difference
that it is unnecessary in my opinion to put one in.
You can have a large field to select from, to make up
a four-dollar grade, as you can get almost all kinds
of material and styles at prices that will allow you
from one dollar to one dollar and a quarter profit
on each pair. Above the four-dollar line, you can
have all prices you may choose ; but be sure that they
possess merit and have something about them to induce the purchaser to invest, and satisfy him well
when he comes to wear them.. Never attempt to make
customers think you are selling at an extremely close
margin by marking your goods, "One dollar and sev-

enteen cents," " Two dollars and five cents," and so on. It is all right for " Cheap John ;" but first-class trade will not take any stock in it. Get a good profit on everything you can. The public will not appreciate you any better if you sell at cost. Seventy-five per cent would think you were getting rich, if you told every one of them that you were losing money on every pair. Now, here is the whole story in a nut-shell ; you have got to have different-priced shoes, and it does not make any difference to the public whether you make twenty-five cents or one dollar on a pair, providing you give them the worth of their money. They cannot tell what a shoe is worth by looking at it, but must take your word for everything. And now comes in a very important point, that must be followed strictly, and that is, never misrepresent an article if you wish to build up a trade and a reputation that will stand. Be honest with your customers ; handle only such makes as you have confidence in, and should a shoe that you have warranted prove poor, the stock crack, and your customer return it to you having worn it but a short time, replace it with a new pair, free of cost. Don't attempt to patch it, as a new shoe with a patch on it is a poor advertisement for your store, and never satisfies the buyer.

In placing your stock on the shelves, keep each manufacturer's goods by themselves as far as possible. See that the cartons are placed squarely one above the other, and that the ends are even. Nothing looks more slovenly than a lot of shoe boxes placed hit or

miss, as it were, on the shelf, one projecting half its
length out, and the next pushed as far in. Mark the
boxes on the end in plain figures, showing kind, last,
size, width and price.

After showing goods always see that they are buttoned up before they are put back in the box, and if
the bottoms are slightly soiled by trying on, clean
with a rubber eraser, and restore the finish by rubbing
with tissue paper or the smooth handle of your long
button-hook. If you follow this plan your goods will
always be ready to show, and you will know just
where to put your hand to get the kind you want.

It hardly seems necessary to advise the proprietor
of a store to be gentlemanly and pleasant with customers. That seems to me to be such an important
part that self-interest would compel him to be ; yet
there are some customers who will try a man's patience most sorely. For instance, after-trying a dozen
or more pairs on a customer, and not making a sale
when you know that several of them have been an elegant
fit, but have been rejected on some frivolous ground,
that is the time to exercise self-control. Never show
that you are put out in the least, but accompany
them to the door and tell them that you are very
sorry you could not give them a fit, and you hope to
have a better assortment next time they call. They
will remember it, and some time you will have the
pleasure of selling them, perhaps, one of the same
styles that they had tried on and rejected before.

If a customer returns a pair of shoes and asks to
have his or her money back, always return it if the

shoes are not soiled or damaged. Never let him suppose for a moment that it makes any difference to you worth speaking of. If you find that you have got some styles on your shelves that don't sell readily at the price marked, and they are likely to become shop-worn, mark them down. If you cannot get cost out of them, sell them for less than cost. It never pays to keep such goods in stock; they take room that salable goods ought to occupy.

Another very important point in sizes. Watch your stock closely, and never allow lines that you intend to handle to be broken in sizes if you can avoid it. I have never found it necessary to keep a stock book and check off the size and style as sold, but it may be a good plan if you have time to attend to it. But it is necessary to keep a sufficient number of books to enable you to know what you are doing, where your cash comes from and where it goes, how much you owe and to whom you owe it. In my own business, I keep two books lying open on my desk. In one I enter all cash transactions, money received and what received for, and all amounts paid out and what paid for. This book is balanced every night. That shows me whether I have omitted to enter any transaction, and enables me to look it up at once and correct. From this the different accounts are entered in the ledger under their proper heads. This book also shows the amount of cash sales for each day, week, month, and the total for the year.

In the other book, I keep a record of every pair of shoes taken from the store and not paid for, and the person's name who has them ; and when they are paid for or returned I check them off, and, if sold, enter the sale in the first book. Take an inventory once every year ; if goods have depreciated in value invoice them at what they are worth at time of invoice, not what they cost you. Do not make a practice of cutting prices. You will surely get found out, and it will injure you more than you make. It also leaves an impression on the mind of the purchaser that you are making fabulous profits, and you can expect to have them repeat the bantering process every time they look at goods in the future.

You will find that advertising if properly done will help your trade by keeping your name and goods in the minds of the public. It will be impossible to tell you just how to advertise, but you may find out by trying different ways, and be able to decide for yourself. Discount your bills if possible. If you cannot, pay promptly as they come due ; but if you find this impossible, write the parties, explain the reason, and ask for an extension, or go to your bank and borrow the amount. That keeps your credit good, and lets your creditors know just when to expect their money.

I also want to say a word about buying from agents. You will not have your store open many days before the "traveling man" will be opening his samples and pouring his wonderful story about the superior merits of his line into your ears. That is his business ; don't blame him for doing it, but don't allow every one of them that calls to induce you to buy. All he wants is a sample order. "One dozen, two dozen, that is not many ; you surely can work that many off." But listen not, for if you do it will result in an accumulation of odds and ends and broken lots ; the salable sizes gone, and the unsalable left on your hands to be sold at a loss. When you find a house that suits you, stick to it. You know what to expect from the goods, and if the firm is a live one they will keep up to times, in style and quality and price.

And now I think I will bring this article to a close. There are many things I might have said, that I have left unsaid. I haven't told you how to run a cheap store because I have no experience in that line of trade. I haven't said anything about rubbers ; but I will say now, if you sell seconds, mark the drawers "second quality," and explain the difference to your customers. Give them to understand that they are cheap in quality, cheap in price, but dear in the end. And now, fellow-workers, I will bid you adieu. Let us work faithfully, earnestly and intelligently, remembering what the "good book" has said : "Seest thou a man diligent in his business, he shall stand before kings, he shall not stand before mean men."

How to Manage a Retail Shoe Store.

BY R. F. W. BACHMAN, NEW ORLEANS, LA.

The trade is under lasting obligations to the RE-CORDER for the wise efforts constantly put forth to bring the shoe business to the proper standard of excellence. Its last happy idea of "How to Manage a Retail Shoe Store" has been duly appreciated, as we have seen by the able essay of Mr. Charles Doney, of Ottawa, Canada, to whom all honor is due—the first prize inclusive—for the courage displayed in writing the introductory essay. And those clever and instructive essays of Messrs. Wm. S. Weld and W. H. Travin—may these gentlemen all live to a ripe old age in peace and plenty.

These admirable essays have prompted me to accept your kind invitation to enter the list for the "leather medal."

Don't for a moment entertain the thought of entering the retail shoe business unless it shall be with the view of making it a success. If this is your idea, the next thought should be, have you sufficient capital? if so, what is the style or character of trade you desire to cater for? Give this subject the most careful study. After matured reflection, the next and all-

important consideration is location, ever remembering that location has fixed value in all branches of
business, and rent is of no consideration where business prospers. Many persons on entering business
have an idea that rent should be the first consideration. I think otherwise, on the maxim that " 'Tis
better to be a dog among kings, than a king among
dogs."

Don't for a moment think of going into business
unless you have the requisite qualifications, and are
fully competent to manage the same. Having these
requirements, you may with safety embark your fortune in the shoe business with some certainty of success, provided also that all else are equal. The essays of the gentlemen above referred to will readily
indicate the line of action you should adopt towards
the patrons of the establishment, and the necessary
arrangements for the successful management of the
store.

Don't lose sight for a moment that a thorough
system of book-keeping (simple and to the point),
and management of accounts also, is an absolute
necessity, without which one would find it a most
difficult matter to keep the "wolf from the door."
An account of stock should be taken once a year, a
trial balance made, the profit and loss account properly considered, and the loss and gain for the year
known. For this reason the taking account of stock
brings most forcibly to your view the character of
your stock. As no man, however good a buyer he
may be, can always find ready sale for all his pur-

chases, hence by taking account he at once sees his error, corrects the same, and avoids, to a certain extent, the repetition of the mistake. First loss is always the cheapest, hence, when he finds an unsalable shoe, he should at once fix a price that will enlist the attention of the public. Keep on reducing the price on this character of stock until the last pair is sold, but as an offset to this reduction on unsalable shoes, there should be a corresponding firmness in the maintenance of prices on regular goods.

Don't have two prices. Make your prices so that they shall be alike satisfactory to your patrons and your support, treating the child like the parent, and your most humble customer as you serve your lordly patron, ever remembering that the poor man's dollar goes as far as the rich man's.

Don't for a moment refuse to take back a pair of shoes for exchange or otherwise, even if the same have been kept out an undue time ; better put up with an inconvenience and even a loss than mar the good-will of your patrons. Don't get angry when shoes are brought to you for being defective—claiming an allowance. Quietly and calmly show them their faults if you can, or make good the loss. It will pay.

Don't keep a dirty store. "A careless master makes poor clerks." Keep the corners clean and everything in its place. Taking account of stock is a valuable assistant in this all-important matter, as it brings all the stock to the front in a clean and salable condition. Don't open your store later than your neigh-

bors, nor close earlier. Have regular hours and stick
to them, and as you cannot delegate all your authority
and wishes to your clerks, it becomes your duty to be
ever watchful of your own interest, always remembering that he who would prosper must to his business
give the strictest attention. The price of success in
any business mainly rests upon untiring energy and
application.

Don't fail to keep a good bank account; by this I
. mean an account that is not harassing to the bank
officers. It will help you amazingly in a direction
least expected. If it is possible, pay cash for your
goods; you will buy on more favorable terms and
be more guarded in your purchases. To the retailers
this is a riddle that many have yet to solve, but it is
the key of success in many an instance, where in
close competition you might otherwise succumb. If
you are prosperous, I beg to remind you to keep
your good fortune to yourself, otherwise you may en-
counter additional competition from a quarter least
expected, as well as cause your neighboring competitors to be envious. Live humbly and quietly in
keeping with your business, which never for a moment lose sight of.

If failing, or your business is not quite satisfactory,
then keep cool, hold your own counsel, and work like
a man to retrieve your condition. But a short time
since, a gentleman who has been doing for many
years a large and prosperous business, all at once discovered that he was in a failing condition, as he supposed. He came to me after having spent a night

in tears, and stated his case. I at once saw that he was excited and in no condition to explain his affairs properly. I got him to go to his store and make up his debtor account in full to date. I at once saw that his expenses had been in keeping with his prosperous days, and far beyond his present ability to meet. I advised him to reduce his store and family expenses at once, and directed his line of action for the time-being, which timely act of friendship resulted in setting him on his feet, and happiness, and I trust. prosperity, has once more entered his home. Go slow; pay as you go; be honest, just and conservative.

Don't try to sell for cash exclusively. It cannot be done successfully, except, perhaps, in large cities like New York and Philadelphia. In the provinces it is different. My impressions are, that as you have the ability so let your business be; always let your judgment dictate your line of action. Cash is a most excellent commodity in its way, but cash buyers you cannot control, however painstaking you are. Cash goes where it pleases, and others sell as cheaply as you. Hence, cash is controlled by no influence whatever save its immediate self. But not so with credit. It brings in its train personal friendship and retention of patronage.

I sell all I can for cash and all I can on credit, and what is more on long credit too. I have ever found the credit system the best paying part of my business; it brings in a line of influence that otherwise I never could have obtained.

Don't try to keep everything that is called for ; for however large your stock or assortment may be, you would, nevertheless, find it an impossibility to fit and please all. Hence I would suggest that you keep such lines as may be found consistent for the well-being of your business. But here lies, perhaps, the secret of success, or the disasters that so often one meets in the retail shoe business, the want of strict attention to minute details, or the keeping of the sizes, etc., of the stock up to date. Too much care cannot be given to this all-important branch of the business. Men after riding on the crest of the wave of success, as the tide comes in, get what is commonly known in the country as the "big head," leave the details of business to their clerks whilst they recreate and bask in the sunshine of ease and indifference. The final result is inevitable. Eternal vigilance and its attending economies is the only road to success, and the shoe business is no exception to the inexorable rule.

Don't for a moment think that advertising can be dispensed with. Judicious advertising is a most wonderful adjunct, without which we can do but little ; but when and where and how to advertise—there lies the rub. Quackery and misrepresentations may for the time-being prosper, but I am impressed with the old-fashioned idea that "Honesty is the best policy," and whatever you publish relative to your business should be in strict accordance with truth. It has paid me, and I think it will pay others too.

Remember also that clerks are human, and although

subordinate they are not menial. Treat them like gentlemen, with kindness and due consideration. In return you will better enlist their attention to the interests of your establishment. They occupy the same position toward you that the organ pumper does to the organ. "No pumper, no music."

Cultivate the closer relations of amity and goodwill with your fellow retail shoe-dealers. Be ever ready and willing to divide profits fairly with them. Whenever they may require selections from your stock, neighborly aminities do much toward making life pleasant and your business profitable. The "gentlemen of the road" should not be forgotten. Their labors and responsibilities are peculiar, and, as a whole, a more pleasant and agreeable set of men cannot be found. Don't, as too many retailers unfortunately do, permit these gentlemen to induce you to be overstocked. Treat them kindly, but study your own interest; buy what you require, no more; do not countermand orders. With manufacturers deal fairly and not with over-exactness. I have ever found them willing and anxious to do right, and as the retailer's duty is to study the interests of his patron, so likewise the interest of the manufacturer is to serve the retailer with fidelity.

And, finally, as for general stores and dry-goods dealers, the world has not been made for one class, but for all. The manufacturer sells to whom he pleases or can; so does the retailer. We can no more control the action of the manufacturer than we can the Mississippi River. Let the dry-goods men do

as they please ; it is their alienable right. If the retailer is alive to his own interest, it makes but little
difference what others do, so long as he attends to
his own immediate concern. The great misfortune is
that man pays more attention to his neighbor's business than he does to his own. In other words, every
man must be the best and sole judge as to the character and style of business he follows. These are my
humble views.

Inasmuch as you have to make good all reclama-
tions, etc., I would most strongly urge that the manufacturer's brand should not be permitted. The retailer, being responsible, should derive all the benefits
from the sales. His name and his only should be
branded on the shoes, otherwise honesty and fair-
dealing are valueless.

How to Manage a Retail Shoe Store.

BY I. B. ARNOLD, CAMPAIGN, ILL., FIRST PRESIDENT OF
THE NATIONAL RETAIL SHOE–DEALERS' ASSOCIATION.

In this communication I shall not attempt fine
language, full-rounded sentences or rhetorical flourish.
The management of a retail store requires other
qualifications. A silvery tongue and flowery language
are valuable endowments, but are not essentials either
for the management of a retail store or a writer on
the subject. Your readers are more interested in the
ideas than the manner in which they are presented.
The limits of a magazine article will permit only the
presentation of salient points. Full information cannot be given on printed pages.

It is hardly possible that two or more persons
should write on this subject without, on some points,
expressing the same ideas ; yet by the majority there
will be great difference of opinion. The experience
of each must, in some measure, differ from others ;
the surroundings are different, education and instruc-
tion are not the same ; the inclination of the mind of
one leads him into a channel diverging from all
others.

The part of the country in which located will have
much to do with the conduct of a store. In a large
city it would differ from a small town ; one in Maine

from one in Texas; Montana from Florida. To make rules to govern or formulate any particular line of procedure would be as difficult as to arrive at a philosophical conclusion upon the family incidents of every domestic day. Rules and system are necessary to success, but he who has many rules and adheres to them rigidly will fail. Conditions change, circumstances differ, and what should be done at one time should be avoided at another. A few simple rules, which shall be overshadowed and sometimes modified by abundant common sense, are the best foundation for good management. Matters of importance, each small in itself, will be presented every hour in the day to which no rule will apply, and with no time for reflection must be decided at once. A business man oftener fails at this point than at any other, or perhaps all others together. To enumerate all these incidents would be to count the stars. Upon judicious decisions depend largely whether your customers are pleased or offended; whether you make sales or lose them, leave a good impression or bad one, succeed or fail. A request may be granted in such manner as to offend, or refused with such grace as to please. To "think twice before you speak" will apply to a buyer, but, except he is a remarkably rapid thinker, will not apply to a retail salesman. A little delay in arriving at a right conclusion often loses your customer, and he is more offended because of the delay, though you may decide in his favor, than if you at once, pleasantly, with expressed regret, refused. Decide at once, and abide the consequences.

The first qualification every manager of a retail store needs is a knowledge of the business, knowledge of how to do business, and be well informed in qualities of leather, details of workmanship, and goods in demand. It is a fact, that often those who believe themselves best informed are those whose experience has been limited to a small line and a few months' time, while the merchant of many years' close application confesses ignorance. In the race for business the man who thinks he knows enough will be left far in the rear by industrious, persevering competitors. In trade, as in science, the sophomores are wise while the Newtons confess ignorance.

Some years ago I took into my store as salesman a bright, smart, intelligent, fairly educated young man of twenty-two. After he had been with me two weeks I one day said to him, "Alfred, how long do you think it will take you to learn this business?" He answered, "I think I can learn it thoroughly in about three months." Some time afterwards I said to him, "You have been in my store four years and are now about to go into another field. You have had every opportunity, much of my assistance, and have done well. What do you think now? He replied, "I have a fair start."

There are hundreds, possibly thousands, of retail dealers in the United States who never had "a fair start." It is true that sometimes a man becomes a good mechanic who never served an apprenticeship, but he has labored under many disadvantages from which his associate who learned the trade in his early years is free.

In location, as well as most other things generally, "the best is the cheapest." The kind of trade expected often makes a location desirable or otherwise. The location best suited to the trade of farmers and mechanics will not necessarily be such as calls the most fine trade. If the design is to keep fine goods mostly or wholly, the place is where other lines of fine goods for ladies are sold, but such a place, with such surroundings, will not necessarily call a class of customers who desire a medium grade. Decide what class you desire, and locate "where they most do congregate."

Of course desirable locations are high-priced, and it is possible to fly too high. A small capital and small stock in a large store which manifests to customers great extremes will cause them to look upon the proprietor with contempt, and all the blandishments he can command only make him appear the more ridiculous. A small store well filled is far better than a large one noticeable for its emptiness. In a large city, a neat, well-kept, small stock of fine goods, often replenished, and always fresh, in a cozy, nicely furnished room, may be profitable. There must, necessarily, be much money invested for the volume of stock.

The most successful shoe-dealers, except a few in th: large cities, are those who in the main carry a medium grade of substantial goods at moderate price, and who cater to the desires of the multitude. Fine trade expects and must have expensive surroundings, extremely affable and polite treatment, and great consideration, for all of which they should and must pay. Such people will not step on Cheapside, though Broadway be thrice the distance and prices proportionally higher. The multitude want all they pay for, and are looking for the place where a little money will buy a large amount of serviceable goods.

There are certain qualities which should be possessed by your salesmen, among which are the following : Good character and unblemished reputation, bright and intelligent, well-informed as to qualities cf goods, familiar with your stock, affable, pleasant, accommodating, judge of human nature (a most important element of success). Know how and when to talk, not too little nor too much. When opportunity permits talk about things in which customers are interested ; business, to business men ; crops, live stock, etc., to farmers ; family and friends, to ladies. A good salesman to ladies is seldom equally so to gentlemen. With few exceptions, both men and women are susceptible to flattery ; to the former it must be used sparingly, judiciously, and strike the weak point, which must be well known. There are many points upon which a mistake can scarcely be made in flattering ladies. Of course it may be overdone. If a lady has a baby don't fail to speak to it ; fondle it, and if the ugliest little human in creation the more will the mother be pleased with such attention. Next to the babies are the other children. Say something pleasing to or about them. If a lady is vain of a small foot, use her vanity. If she has a large one, and is sensitive about it, speak about how many shoes you sell larger than hers. If a mercenary motive is discovered, or an injudicious sentence uttered, the case is hopeless. In general, gentlemen will stand a little flattery, ladies much. If administered judiciously, the effect is remarkable; but the slightest over-dose is nauseating.

I have said intelligence is a qualification. Do not mistake college education for intelligence. All the information in college text books will never qualify a man for business. Observation has shown that for success in business the man with a common school education, much knowledge of the world and human nature, outstrips the man of high literary and scientific attainments almost without effort. A shrewd business man once said to me, "I desire no better fortune than to be surrounded by college men with money." There are exceptions. I should not object to a salesman because he was classically educated, but I should not consider it an important qualification.

I would not be understood to disparage literary education; far from it. I desire all my children to take a course in college; at the same time I hope to teach them that a knowledge of men and things is fully as important as all they gain from text books; that after they leave college it will not be going downward to be employed as a salesman in any reputable business.

Treat your employes with consideration. Deserve their good opinions.

Keep an exact account of your business transactions. Recently I adopted a system which has proved very satisfactory. I have little books of which the following is a copy of a page :

Boots and Shoes.....		Boots and Shoes......	
Rubbers............... 300		Rubbers............... 300	
Findings............... 3		Findings.... 3	
Cobbling.............		Cobbling	

Each of these books contains one hundred leaves, is consecutively numbered, and a certain number of books are numbered for each clerk ; the clerk also has a figure (a letter may be substituted) to designate him and his books from others. The figure 3 shown designates the clerk. The figures 300 one of the consecutive numbers. The figure 3 will appear on every ticket used by this clerk. The first book will be from 1 to 100 inclusive ; the second 101 to 200 ; third from 201 to 300, and so on. Each page contains a ticket and duplicate numbered exactly alike and perforated as shown. When a sale is made and the cash received, the clerk hands the ticket with the cash to the cashier, who makes the change, puts the amount of the sale in the drawer, and the ticket on the spindle. The left hand or duplicate remains in the book until evening. If the goods are to be charged the name of the purchaser is written at the bottom ; the items are written on the back of the ticket and the amount on the face opposite its class (boots and shoes, rubbers, findings, cobbling). An account is kept with each class, and each night the total sold during the day is properly entered. Also the amounts sold for cash and on credit. Thus each class shows for itself, and much valuable information is obtained. Each clerk has the duplicates of all tickets he has used during the day, and his tickets must tally with those on the spindle. He is credited with making the amount of sales his tickets show. Each night at closing, the clerks tear out all duplicate tickets of the day's sale and give them to the pro- prietor. The amount of cash tickets together with the amount paid in on ledger account are the total cash receipts. These books cost me seven dollars and fifty cents per hundred not numbered. I have a consecutive numbering stamp which I use and num ber the books as required.

In purchases, a dealer must be governed by his customers' wants ; but there are some rules, though axioms, we often forget. "Do not buy what you do not want because it is cheap." "Do not buy because others do." Salesmen tell to whom they have sold as an argument why you should buy. It is well to give this the credit it merits, but you must consider difference in circumstances, desires of customers, stock cn hand, and numerous other things which weigh more than the opinions of Smith or Jones.

It is often said, "You ought to be satisfied to do as well as your neighbors." This is the worst kind of an argument. Your neighbors may all be doing badly, and certainly the majority will die poor. You must do better than your neighbors, get out of the beaten track of your grandfathers, and push your way to success.

Be particular to order such goods as you need; make a complete memorandum of style, quality and price; don't reject goods without sufficient cause, but don't accept them too far off sample. Your experience has shown that such goods are always a damage to you. Don't buy too many kinds; don't try to keep a stock of every kind any customer may ask for. Don't invest too much money in goods asked for once a month which leaves you too little for staples wanted every day.

These days much is said about the value of cash purchases, and you are told to buy for cash, get the discount, make a name as a cash buyer, etc.

I would not for one moment detract from any of these arguments, but I am reminded of what President Lincoln said when he was told how necessary it was to pay the national debt, which was then large. "Yes, pay it, pay it. It is as easy to pay a large debt as a small one when you have no money." Let me whisper in your ear that very few men, fewer than you suppose, have money with which to cash all their bills. Pay cash when you can, use credit judiciously for the balance. Do not believe that because you are not a capitalist you cannot do business.

When you get a bargain, do not give it away. Do not mark your goods in all cases an exact percentage on cost. If for any reason you have bought a lot of goods for less than regular price, add the difference to your profit. Your losses will be larger than all such differences. Sell for fair profits except where competitors cause you to cut on certain lines. On well-known goods sell as low as your competitors until they sell for less than cost, when you must manage secretly to buy their stock. Your customers have no regard for your pecuniary interest, and will not be thankful if you sell them goods at half cost, but if they fail you will be censured just as severely as though you had sold them at fair prices. Give them good articles, and make them pay you living profits.

Here again comes the consideration of the cash system. Whether it is best or not depends on location and surroundings. While in many cases the cash system is best, credit has many points in its favor.

Arguments in favor of cash are on every hand. Credit has few advocates even among those who practice it. I am of the opinion that in small cities and towns, a system which shall in no case exceed one-third credit, leaving more than two-thirds cash, is best. Let credits be discreet, short, usually not exceeding thirty days. Collect sharp, extend the time to deserving cases, say *no* where there is a doubt, and at the end of the year you will have small losses and more business than a strictly cash house similarly located. Customers will buy more goods and say less about price on credit than for cash. This system will leave comparatively little on your books, all bills small, and give you the prestige of desiring to accommodate your customers. Be sure to insist on periodical settlements, usually monthly. Be lenient to those who for good reasons cannot pay promptly; but let them understand that you do so to accommodate, and make an exception to your rule in their favor. Insist on definite times for payment.

Do not let farmers betray you into selling goods and making bills payable after they sell their grain. "After harvest" means after the grain is cut, stacked, threshed, stored, price suits, it is sold, delivered, paid for; and if no other use is found for the money, you will be paid, but that may be thirty days or nine months. You may be generous to your customers, but you must be just to yourself.

Advertising is a matter to which dealers generally pay too little attention. Not that they advertise too little, for I believe an unnecessary amount of money is usually paid for it. To simply say " I. B. Arnold, dealer in boots, shoes and rubbers, 19 Main street, Campaign, Ill., largest stock, lowest prices," continuing indefinitely with like generalities, may do me a little good, but is not that stereotyped? The reader turns from such an advertisement, disgusted. Use some novelty to call attention. Mention advantages and special good qualities of your goods better than others. You must induce customers to call at your store to see goods because they are superior to those offered elsewhere for same price or equal to them at a lower price. Not only so, but you must give plausible reasons, and have goods that will justify them.

The most foolish of all advertising is to make misstatements and laud articles or qualities beyond their

· merits. When a customer discovers that your advertisement has deceived him, he is lost to you probably for all time. On this point, as well as all others, it pays to be candid. Be honest, be truthful.

Sell your own goods. Do not bind yourself to any manufacturer or jobber by advertising and selling goods with such manufacturer's or jobber's name thereon. A time may come when you will desire to drop that line of goods, and take another. If you have allowed yourself to use said names, when you drop the goods your competitor may take them, and you thereby put a club in his hands with which to beat your head. Of goods that have a national reputation it may be policy to have a few to show and sell when you can sell no others; but, as a rule, let your goods be stamped with your name or none. Make your name a recommendation. If you desire specialties, adopt a name not used by any other dealer for each, and have the goods stamped as you desire; advertise the merits and establish a reputation for each kind; be not bound to anybody. You can change when you choose; change or retain names as seems most to your advantage. Do not forget that if any jobber or manufacturer advertises for you, he must be paid for it. I know manufacturers do not favor this, but "self-preservation is the first law of nature."

The matter of letting goods out on approval I was inclined to pass, because of a most unpleasant subject whose difficulties I have never been able to solve. I have never met a dealer who could get over it easily.

It is well to say, "If they are damaged, don't take them back except at a discount," but if you are politic you often do—I do, because it is the best way out of it. When goods are returned damaged, not paid for, what are you to do? Grit your teeth and smile. What else can you do? If you have a strictly cash system you must return money where goods come back, and to certain customers you must yield. This is a case where rigid rules cannot be observed. An uncertain amount of damage must be pocketed, gracefully or otherwise, and is one of the numerous "ills" the shoe-dealer "is heir to."

Sell your goods for one price. Your customers will be better pleased, and in the end you will have the most satisfactory business.

Welcome customers cordially; make them feel "at home," but do not permit loafing.

Keep your goods well arranged and neatly packed. The use of single-pair boxes for all but coarse and heavy goods is advisable. Let your store be a model of cleanliness and order.

Do not show too many goods; but every customer expects to see more than one pair.

Consider the advice of all, but do as seems to you best. He who has never retailed shoes is most likely to give advice and show you a way out of each difficulty, as every quack has a nostrum for the most serious and complex disease.

Join the Retail Boot and Shoe Dealers' Association, assist in promoting its most laudable objects, and while so doing gain a hundred times its cost for yourself.

How to Manage a Retail Shoe Store.

BY HECTOR N. McDONALD, TIVERTON, ONT., CANADA.

If this essay be of sufficient merit for publication in the RECORDER, the reader will please bear in mind that the experience and observation of the writer has been devoted exclusively to the retailing of boots and shoes in small towns and villages, and whose customers have been mostly country people. Hoping the sentiments that I advance will be amusing to city dealers, and call the criticism or approval of retailers in like situation, I proceed to express what I have experienced as the best mode in dealing with the people of this locality.

First of all, we must bear in mind that our success depends on the present demand. And we know there is only a certain demand for everything. It is in supplying some one particular demand we find the grand object of our usefulness, and he that contributes the most and the best for the least charge is the most enviable.

One of nature's grandest laws is its rewards, the greatest being given to those who most successfully adapt their services to the general need. It should, therefore, be our highest ambition to supply the de-

mand with sufficient quantity, combined with the
very best quality for the least money that we can
with safety, allowing ourselves proper remuneration
for our services over and above necessary expenses,
including interest of capital invested. The proper
quantity of boots and shoes that should be kept in
stock should only be sufficient to supply the demand
that we may under all circumstances and probabili-
ties be called upon to supply. In these days of pro-
gressive railways and prompt deliveries an excess of
the necessary quantity would be precarious to safety.
As it is very important to keep in stock a good assortment of all the prevailing styles and kinds most
suitable to the requirements of our customers in each
season of the year, our aim should be to keep ourselves watchful of all inventions of new styles or improvements in contour, material or workmanship, that
may be made public through the medium of trade
papers or advertisements, so as, if suitable, to be the
first to introduce them in the locality.

The quantity of footwear to place on the shelves,
which I find pleases the average customer the most,
is no less than three pairs of each size throughout all
the kinds in demand. Most customers on entering a
shoe store are pleased to see the shelves well filled
with a choice selection of fresh and handsome looking boots and shoes. And whatever size and style
they call for we can promptly set before them two or
three pairs to choose from, especially to those who
are disposed to consider their own judgment of
more importance in the selection of footwear. An-

other important feature that should receive our careful attention is to keep nothing but boots and shoes of the very best quality, and at every opportunity to educate the people to know the difference between a cheap shoddy shoe, and one made of solid leather throughout. We will notice that in most cases the customer will admit that the most serviceable will be the cheapest, and of course, to be able to teach, the dealer must be "master of the situation." The more thoroughly a dealer is acquainted with the manufacture of both leather and shoes, the greater advantage he has over his competitors in both buying and selling.

It should be our constant study to be as thorough in the knowledge of our calling as possible. And we can obtain a great deal of information in the art of tanning and dressing of the different kinds of shoe leather by studying the excellent books now published on this subject. As to the manufacture of boots and shoes, it seems to me, that one of the necessary accomplishments a dealer should be desirous of, is to have served a good long apprenticeship on the shoe bench, repairing and making boots and shoes. This mechanical skill, with intel igent adaptation to the requirements of the shoe business, I consider as one of the grandest qualifications necessary in a dealer.

In every shoe business there are always more or less soiled or shop-worn shoes, that by a mechanical dealer could be made as good as new by simply treeing and dressing them ; of the coarser kinds, perhaps a retrimming of heels and edges, buffing the bottoms, and then giving them a good treeing and dressing, would be necessary. The improvement in appearance and selling qualities would profitably pay for the time expended. The more or less shop-worn shoes on hand is in proportion to the acquaintance a dealer has with the manufacture of shoes and lea·her. In the buying, a dealer of these qualities would with certainty know whether such a shoe would remain on the shelves until it became soiled with frequent handling or trying on. There is always some defect in articles that have been rejected by the customers, which would not have escaped the careful examination that a dealer of this kind exercises in the purchasing of boots and shoes.

After the receipt of the goods it would be wise to carefully examine every shoe, so that every lack or flaw may be properly adjusted before' offering them to the public. Those excellent inventions of iron counter lasts are indispensable in a shoe store, especially when the present lasting tacks are so much in use. Occasionally some trouble is experienced with the channel nails that are improperly clinched in the toes of shoes. They can be easily removed by simply raising the channel with a sharp peg awl, then peg out the nail far enough to catch it with the nippers, then cement the channel as before.

In the arranging of boots and shoes on the shelves, great care should be taken to keep every kind and size in its allotted place, so, whatever size and style is called for, it can be instantly presented. If shelf boxes are used we should procure those that are as attractive in appearance as possible, with a neatly designed label in front showing the style of the contents. Boxes should nicely fit the shelves, and be deep enough to allow the shoes to stand upright in them, which will preserve the finish and contour much better than by doubling them in order to place them in boxes that are too shallow. Another important requisite that should receive our careful attention is cleanliness. We cannot be too particular in keeping the store as tidy and clean as possible, as dust is very injurious to leather. I believe that a dealer doing a large business, in a city or town, would find it profitable to have a competent employe whose special duty would be to attend to the order and cleanliness of the store.

We should consider the floor space between the counters as belonging to the public, and in our care. We should, therefore, keep it clean, and clear of all packing boxes, goods, or anything, except public furniture such as good easy stools or chairs, and perhaps a handsome lounge, a mirror, or anything that will be comfortable and home-like to the customers. Sufficient space should be separated by a screen to be reserved for customers in trying on boots or shoes. And directly in front of the screen place a nice show-case with samples of ladies' and children's fine wear.

I regard that the subject of light should receive some careful study. We know that by examining a shoe in the sunlight we can very easily see any defects in finish, material, or workmanship ; then, the

proper degree of light should be just short of where
the defects of the shoe begin to show. The more
perfect the goods are, the stronger the light may be,
and only experiments and observations can arrive at
the proper light most advantageous to the selling of
boots and shoes.

Allowing the light to be as cheerful as possible, we
should never allow any unpleasant reflection or direct
rays of the sun to enter the store. Nothing is more
injurious to boots and shoes than a too warm and
dry atmosphere, especially rubber goods. Rubber
goods should be kept near the floor in the coolest
part of the store.

In turning our attention to the buying of boots and
shoes, we come to the rock on which the dealer
bases his main hope of success, and certainly the
rock on which has been wrecked the aspirations of
many inexperienced dealers. To a great extent our
success depends mostly on our shrewdness and ability
in buying well. In buying, let us consider ourselves
as buying agents in the employ of the public, for
surely we are the servants of the public, and our re-
ward will be in proportion to the value they receive
for their money. Since the public places the most
confidence in the dealer who possesses the best judgment, and the highest intelligence in the selection
and buying of boots and shoes, we should also be
particular to buy none but those of the very best
quality, and only buy as few grades as will supply the
demand. In order to do so it is desirable that we
should be well acquainted with the productions of the

different makers, by either examining the samples of traveling salesmen, or visiting the factories of the best-known makers. If we consider the prices of certain houses too high for the class and quality of the goods, it is much better to say so plainly and firmly, than to try to beat the prices down by offering less, because any house that offers goods at one price, and, in case we refuse, offers them for less, cannot be recommended to any one. We shoul l always pay cash for our purchases, thus securing discounts and other advantages that cash buyers have over those who buy on credit, and in all our buying we should made it a rule never to quote the prices of one house to another.

Retailing for cash has sufficient advantages over the credit system, both to the retailer and customer, to warrant to a great extent the success of a business that strictly adheres to this system, for it is reasonable to suppose the public will deal where they will get the full value of their money, rather than where they only get part value in goods, the balance going to pay expenses connected with book-keeping, and probably the bad debts of others.

A cash business may therefore be commended : First, for its economy, requiring less expense for book-keeping, fewer clerks and less risks connected with crediting doubtful customers ; second, for its fairness, as all pay cash, one price only is required. While crediting, justice requires that he who pays cash should have some corresponding reduction in price below what is charged to him whose pay is doubtful. And, last, the cash business is to be commended for its comparative safety, and chances of successfully competing with those who give credit. Since the farming community has always a certain amount of income through the summer months by the selling of live stock and by the dairy, it is quite possible to have strictly cash business. In these days of sharp competition, it is the dealer's constant study to find means whereby he may reduce expenses and risks, so that he can undersell his neighbor, and of course the cash business has the greater advantage. In a country shoe business that strictly adheres to the one-price cash system, the per cent of profit to be placed on the goods should be the same on all classes and grades. The advantage of this system is that of knowing the exact amount of the expenses per day. We can, on adding up the day's sales, know to a cent the amount of the day's gain. Some advocate that we should have larger profits on the goods that may soon become unfashionable or out of season, In my experience I find that there should be less profit on these than any other, so as to dispose of them before they become unfashionable or out of season. The rate of profit to levy on the goods should bear a relation to the expenses and sales. We should, therefore, know to a cent the amount of our business expenses, and be contented with a fair remuneration for our services and capital. We should conform our private living to style of living of our customers. When we adopt a style of living and expenditure far beyond the reach of our customers, it often creates a feeling among them that we are making too much profit out of them, which reacts injuriously to our trade. The aggregate of our total expenses, including those of our private living, should not exceed one-half of the gross profits of the business. We should, therefore, study economy of the expenses rather than the enlarging of the profits, for probably more fortunes are made by a saving economy in expenses than are made by large profits. We cannot be too particular in our acquaintance with the progress of the business, so that we may notice the very first beginning of the downward tendency in the customary amount of business done. As soon as we notice the decline, we must study out the cause of it. If through less energy and enterprise, we must make an extra effort to increase the sales by every means possible. Whatever the cause may be, it should at once receive our attention. In marking the selling prices on the goods, care should be taken to write the figures very plainly, so there may be no danger of mistaking them. We should also designate by some price mark the date of purchase. Perhaps the most convenient would be the number of the month and the latter figure of the year. If bought in June, 1886, use the figures 66. In marking them thus we should make a rule never to allow the interest of money invested in the shoe to become more than the profit levied.

We should compel every shoe to return its share over cost to the proprietor of the business. Six months is long enough for any shoe to live in the store, and, using proper prudence in our purchases, it is quite unnecessary to keep boots and shoes any longer.

The extent to which a business may be profitably advertised is a matter that can only be governed by what advantages we have over our competitors. If we can justly claim that our goods are superior in quality, or by our business capabilities obtained especial advantages in the purchasing, or greater economy in living and store expenses, by which we can sell cheaper, then of course it would be profitable to advertise extensively. But when we have none of the advantages, the result can only be injurious. As soon as the public ascertain the falsity of the statements we advertise, we cannot expect them to treat us with their patronage. Much lies in the character of the article to be advertised. If it is a patented shoe, for instance, or a special shoe made by a well-known maker, or if the shoe is peculiarly adapted to supply a special demand of the community, and providing there is sufficient profit, either present or prospective, to warrant the expenses incurred, advertising, of course, should be sufficiently extensive to bring the information to the notice of those most likely to be customers. In the form and method of advertising we should study to originate new ideas and improvements on the methods adopted by others, and never to be content to copy even the most intelligent and prosperous of our competitors.

The next feature in importance to judiciously written advertisements, is the art of window dressing.

It requires no small degree of skill to be proficient in this art, bearing in mind the fact that the prime object in the artistic display in show windows is to attract the attention of the public. We should, therefore, make it as attractive as possible. People, in general, are quick to notice any change in the usual order of things, and should the order of things be ever so pleasing, after it becomes usual it fails to attract the notice and comments of the public, therefore constant novelty and change are necessary to secure public attention.

We can measure the degree of ingenuity, taste and inventiveness that a merchant possesses by the display and attractiveness of his show window. If the position of the store faces the sun in any part of the day, the windows should be sufficiently protected by awnings, so as to keep the contents of the window cool and the view complete. We should never hang shoes outside the door, because dust and dry winds are very injurious to leather. The common practice of lighting show windows after night seem to me not to give justice to the display of the contents. I mean putting lamps in such positions that the light shines directly in the faces of the public on the street. How often we can see better with the illumination directly in front of the window than on the goods in the window. Let the town corporation light the street, and let us study to concentrate the light on the goods, so that the view may be pleasing to the public. To accomplish this, I think the better way would be to frost or nicely paint the upper half of the window, and fasten the light directly inside the painted part, and by means of reflectors reflect the light directly on the goods in the window. In this position the public would be, as it were, in the shade, and of course in the most perfect position to view the goods with convenience.

Now we come lastly to the grand object which the retailer should perpetually strive to accomplish in the most perfect manner. This is selling the goods, for a failure in this is a failure in all. An accomplished salesman is born, not made. Good salesmen are naturally endowed with the functions of intelligence and urbanity to a large degree. The former adopts actions and words, most proper to the occasion, to read the characteristics and dispositions of each customer, so that he can say and act the right thing at just the right time. The latter is to perfect the former with politeness, courtesy and pleasantness, in conjunction with friendship, to be enabled to make friends and then retain them.

They also require firmness and decision, in order to politely refuse credit to those to whom even credit should not be given. It is always more pleasant to a customer on entering a store to be promptly met in a pleasant and polite way, than to be met with coldness and lack of courtesy. Cautiousness should be used to see that on'y anxiety enough is shown to please and satisfy the customer that we are trying to give satisfaction to. To show too much anxiety creates a suspicion in the mind of the customer that we are seeking only the benefit of ourselves. If a customer should persist in buying shoes that we know the fit or quality of will not give the comfort and satisfaction necessary in the occupation to which he intends wearing them, we will guard ourselves from future attack by telling him that it is our opinion he will not receive satisfaction or comfort or wear, and that we can supply him with better. We should, before all customers and under all all circumstances, assume an even temper and pleasantness. We should have complete control of our temper, and especially avoid getting into an argument, even though satisfied that the customer is wrong. I have known salesmen to make it a rule never to contradict a customer in anything. They deemed it better wisdom to state their opinion in such a way that the customer will be convinced in his own mind, if not openly, that the salesman thoroughly understands what he says.

In trying to effect a sale, it is much better to speak of the merits than of the cheapness of its price. It is also desirable to have a good memory, so as to remember details, and, as far as possible, former transactions of customers. These are my ideas, and they should be united with an everlasting desire to become educated in the sciences and arts of our honorable calling that may be, from time to time, expressed through the columns of the RECORDER.

How to Manage a Retail Shoe Store.

BY CHARLES HANN, MONTGOMERY, ALABAMA.

"I kind of thought" I would write an article on the subject of "How to Manage a Retail Shoe Store," more as a pleasure than otherwise, as I do not pretend to be capable of competing with such gentlemen as will probably come forward.

Anyway, to start with, a suitably situated and attractive store room with plenty of light and well ventilated is very important. Sometimes location makes or unmakes a man. If catering for a fine trade, don't put up where the cheap trade goes, and vice versa. If for all classes, as I do (being in a small city), try and obtain a location that will take them all in.

Then I would say, especially if your firm name is a long one or hard to pronounce, give your store a name. My store **is** known as the "Red Star Shoe Store." I have the entire front of my building painted white, with about fifty large red stars scattered over it, which created quite a sensation when first seen. That makes my store distinctly known and the best advertisement I have ever had. Besides, it looks grand.

Show windows! Ah! there you can show yourself, and nothing adds more than clean windows and tastefully arranged goods therein. What material to use on the floor of same, and what fixtures, and how to place them. Creating designs, sometimes adding automatic toys about Christmas, putting in a tree, and various other things will produce an admiration and consequent talk in your favor. One of my windows I made a regular stable of, and put a small Shetland pony in. That drew immensely. Then, again, I have found that a handsome doll is an effective advertisement.

As to shelving, I would say, have a cabinet maker do the work, and have it so as to be easily and quickly moved when occasion requires. Mine is in sections made about nine years ago, when twelve-pair cartons were in their glory. It has five shelves divided in spaces holding three cartons, a protruding ledge at the bottom to set boxes on. Underneath that I have two rows of drawers. The whole is painted a light color, in imitation of ash wood. I have moved it four times. The last move I made we sold goods in one store at 7 P. M., and were ready for trade at 7 o'clock the next morning in our new store. Of course we worked all night.

Individual cartons being now almost exclusively used, if wanting new shelving I should have the spaces a little different, but mine does so well, I have never considered a change necessary. I have never used counters until the last year, but would not now be without them. The back part of the store should receive no mean consideration, but have shelving across or in some other manner arranged, so that, when the eyes of your customers look back, it will compare favorably with other parts of the room. Nice low settees or lounges with rugs in front of them, and stools or hassocks for clerks to sit on, are needed for fitting purposes. One or two show-cases will also do their part in beautifying the interior of your store.

Now we will consider the important factor in my estimation—the buying of stock. My thoughts are every day on buying. If I get the right goods, at the proper time, I consider it very little trouble to sell, and I place all other matters as mere auxiliaries. There are some maxims not worth much. "Goods well bought are half sold" is one though that is worth gold eagles to those who follow its silvery path. I am very conservative in buying. Before going East, I prepare myself for just what I want, and try not to deviate from that in the least. How long do you think I figured on how many to buy, what styles, what sizes and widths, of my fine shoes? Just one week. It will take me a month to put in my little book all that I expect to buy, but when I get through with that, no old stock will get into my store. I have a book, wherein I keep manufacturers' names. I have them classified as "Ladies' Fine Shoes," "Ladies' $2 Shoes," "Men's $3 Shoes," and so on. I may want men's hand-sewed shoes. I look over the pages devoted to them, consisting of about forty names, and select whichever one I think will suit me best in the shoe that I want. In that way I have accumulated information that is of incalculable benefit. When I go into the market, I have partly determined plans, where and of whom I will buy, but I work like a beaver, find out all I can, and if I can do better, throw those overboard that I had contemplated patronizing.

I try to let no social courtesies make me forget my duty, which is to buy as cheap as the next one, to get as much wearing quality as possible for the money, and goods that will sell at sight. I will tell you how I keep my stock. One side of the store has ladies' and men's goods. The other side has boys', youths', misses' and children's. I have a certain number of spaces for each. I start with the finest grades and then the next until the grades end. I also start with the largest sizes, and continue them down, so that a clerk can go to a certain space and tell in a minute just what he has to show. When goods come in they are first counted, then examined and marked both cost and selling price, also mate numbered. This latter prevents selling mismates. I do not believe in having uniform cartons. The manufacturers send you nice ones in which to leave your goods, and all hands will quickly discern by a glance where the article is that is wanted, as the mind, through the eye, will soon connect the shoes with the relative boxes. Each side of my store has two clerks, those clerks divide the side in two, each therefore has his position to look after in a l the little details.

I have not fifty dollars' worth of old stock in my whole establishment, and neither need any one else have, but I venture to say, there are not many but have a goodly pile of it. Of course I am extremely cautious, but why not be? If you buy right, no old stock will accrue. Is that not worth striving for?

A few words in reference to dry-goods stores, competition and advertising.

That the dry-goods dealers keeping shoes do harm to the specialty trade of some is a fact. Were it not so, the writer of this would probably be pecuniarily much better off. But what moral right have we to covet what they have as much right to as we? We must cope with them, that is all. They are, I believe, better business people than we are, and their success is due to many things that we give no thought to. For instance, advertising. How many shoe men advertise? and when they do, how do they do it?

I have never seen the advertisements of half a dozen shoe men that were worth the space they occupied in the newspaper. The dry-goods man heads his advertisement with something readable, then follows the style of the article with price therefor. If he has something special it is mentioned. If he has a bargain, likewise. How different from the old, hackneyed style of a shoe man, when he does venture out.

Care should be exercised in procuring help. Honesty, courtesy, cleanliness, knowledge of shoes and general adaptability, not fearing work, are attributes that a clerk should be endowed with.

The credit system is bad. You may tell it to men a hundred times over, however. The hungry desire to

sell will not let them believe it until having under-
gone its sad experience.

A dealer should be insured against fire for an
amount that would cover at least two-thirds of his
stock. Economy should never curtail your lighting
at'night, as an ill-lit store looks too much like sitting
up with a corpse. A few dollars in rent should never
tempt one to move. If you have a good stand, stick
to it ; if not, move by all means ; but remember your
customers will not all move with you.

As to customers, I believe it is a poor policy to
misrepresent goods, as one person treated that way
may deter many others from simply paying you a
visit.

Another prominent mistake that dealers make, is
in trying to sell a customer an article different and
for more money than he wants. How would you
like to go into a cigar store to buy a cigar, and, wanting one for five cents, the dealer should say, "Here are
some nice ones for ten cents. We don't sell many
five-centers any more." Then again should any one
become dissatisfied and return his shoes, wanting the
money, give it to him cheerfully, and it will pay you
twofold. A merchant should strive to wound no
one's feelings, as thereby he gains a popularity worth
money. A proprietor should as much as possible
meet every customer, and, if nothing more, say good
morning or evening, as the case may be, some such
courtesy being expected as an acknowledged appre-
ciation of their custom. Buy no more than you can
pay for in thirty or sixty days. You will be aston-

ished with how little you can do ; you will have no vexatious notes becoming due, which cause sometimes endless troubles, and instead you will be made happy with the discount coupons. How can you fail, if such a course you pursue?

A few words as to office matters, and I am done. My books consume about a half-hour of my time daily. I keep a synoptic, wherein my cash account is posted, merchandise, expenses and my own accounts are kept. The cash is balanced daily, what's posted is transferred to the ledger, and that's about all the book-keeping necessary for any retail store. I keep an account with a bank, and check whenever I choose. That makes the cash easily handled, well taken care of, and my checks are vouchers should I not have a receipt and be called upon the second time to pay a bill. I keep also an invoice and receipt book. All of these are kept in a small but good iron safe in my office, which is in the rear part of the store, where quiet reigns. In the front of the store, one of the counters has a cash drawer, to which there is one key, which I always manipulate, except when away, and then it is intrusted to a trusted salesman.

On the same counter is a small writing desk, wherein the sales are kept, also the cost. Knowing my daily expenses, I can thereby tell just what I am making or losing each day. I have tried to cover all the points I know of, and while not expiating as fully as I might have done, and explaining more explicitly, I feel as if I have devoured enough space and time.

How to Manage a Retail Shoe Store.

BY JAMES H. QUINLAN, MERIDEN, CONN.

To the spectator on a warm day in June, looking in at a shoe store of about $3,000 or $4,000 capital invested, and comprising a man, boy and a peculiar looking artist in a far-off corner, a rather round foot-ball appearance hammmering on something, to look in and see this proprietor sitting in a vacuous reverie, and apparently nothing to do, would lead the looker-on to suppose that this shoe dealer, and shoe dealers in general, had a very easy time of it, and that, in fact, it was a beautiful way to make an easy living. Some years ago this dealer was left a legacy of $5,000 and, liking the appearance of keeping a shoe store, with high hopes, good health and courage, confidence in his fellowmen, but very little business experience, he invested his money in ladies' B's, C's, D's, E's, F's, FF's, EE's, M. S., and a few other letters, and in gents' from 6 to 10, 3, 4, 5 and 6 widths, M. S., hand-sewed, standard screw, hand-turned, etc., and with a modest investment set sail as a shoe retailer. After a few days some customer asked him for something he did not have, so he bought a line of that and a dozen of something else. So for the first two months he was buying until his money was about all invested, and in three months he found he had one good line that would sell rapidly on small profits. Two or three ladies' lines of shoes of different grades of prices seemed to stick to the shelves, for some, being too dear for his class of customers, others of too heavy material, more not well-fitting, he had poor success in his sales. Being an honest, confiding fellow, he left too great a proportion of his book and cash accounts to his clerk. His credit customers began very small at first, but gradually swelled to one-half his business.

By the way, on credit; it is very amusing (if not to the shoe dealer) to the student of human nature to note the various and subtle ways of getting credit. The common way is to pay once or twice and then to be short at the next purchase, or part short, say one-half dollar, to come promptly and pay that then, get credit for one dollar, and gradually double the credit until it amounts to ten dollars, and then disappear or trade somewhere else. The well-dressed lady who did not expect to buy shoes this morning and was one dollar short of the amount, gives her address and promises you a large patronage. Send in your bill a month afterwards and the people in that vicinity don't know her, etc. And the young lady that lives out, coming into the store with nice, richly-dressed children, wants a pair of shoes, fits herself, and leaves the old ones to be repaired. She is to be paid her monthly wages in eight or nine days, and you would oblige her so much. She calls in three weeks, gets her repaired shoes and will pay by Saturday. When

you call with the bill, the lady of the house with
some little effort remembers her and that (very em-
phatically) she was paid every cent and left. And
still it is very hard to do a cash business.

But to return to our subject. My hero found that
one-half his business was on the credit plan, and at
the end of the year one-fourth of it was all he could
collect. The next year he made desperate efforts to
make his business successful. He bought heavily,
advertised freely and gave credit, afraid he would lose
a large part of his trade by refusing, and hoping that
his customers would pay up all back balances. He
sold out in the February of the third year, and placed
himself with that class of a great many that go into
business. This is one way to manage a shoe store
and as a failure it seems to be very successful.

About a year after this a party of friends, your
obedient being of the number, went on an excursion,
and coming to our terminus we saw some workmen
unloading freight cars of lumber. My assigned or
sold-out shoe dealer was balancing a twenty foot
plank preparatory to throwing it off. When I saw
him, leaving my friends, I hailed him. "Ha, there,
working for a change?" "Hallo! yes, and something else, my board also." Then he seemed to get
displeased at my seeing him and went on with his
work. I found him where he boarded, and went to
see him in the evening. He told me some incidents
about himself; how he left where he was doing business with scarcely any money after settling all claims,
disgusted with everybody, business and himself; how

he tried hard to go as a traveling salesman, to get a
book-keeper's position, or salesman in a store, and for
some circumstance or another he was unsuccessful
until finally his money was all gone, then his best
clothes, and finally a tramp. Then made up his mind
to work at anything till he could fix himself up a little, humble himself to some opulent old acquaintance
and with his influence get something of a position.
His health was good, he felt the inclination and had
the courage to begin. I left him with respect. In
two weeks after he got a position in a shoe factory,
and a well-to-do relation told him if he would save
$500 that he would give a loan of $1,000 or so to go
in his old business. He did so. Today he carries
$5,000 to $10,000 stock, and is reputed to be well
off.

When I made up my mind to engage in the shoe
business I called on him. A wet night in December,
I remember it well. Trade was dull and we sat
around the store. I asked him what ideas he had
formed and what resolutions made to make the business a success. "Well, sir," he answered, "One motive was determined pride not to fail. This idea kept
me ever on the alert ; also the experience of my past
mistakes. I selected the location with care where
the business and people were tiding towards most,
kept a well-lighted, inviting and cheerful looking
store ; bought gradually new lines, that is, knowing
that they will fit and wear well, and knowing that they
will not show unseemly *wrinkles* in the vamp when
trying on, studied and learned the taste, style and

price that will suit my customers before I bought
heavy. Why, dear boy, I can tell the exact fit and
measurement of over 100 of my customers now as
they come in, and remember at once the size shoe
they bought last. When you are certain of two or
three lines of men's and ladies' shoes that fit well,
wear well, and the price reasonable, they are bound
to·sell, and you may safely have three or four pairs of
a size in the season. If there is a line of shoes you
want to supersede with a new and better selling shoe,
get in your new line, give the old line the preference
in selling, but, in case you are afraid of losing the
sale, bring on a pair from your reserved new line.

"It takes too long to describe the beautiful accomplishments of a good salesman. I could not explain
it all myself even if I was a good talker. Then I
employ no one without precaution as to their integ-
rity, and use any intuition I may possess once in a
while to test their delicate sense of honesty. Its
poor policy to throw temptation in silver dollars too
carelessly loose to clerks of luxurious tastes. I give
but very little credit. Credit I have found out is
poor business ; it don't pay to collect. The amount
of credit you give depends on what capital you command, but never promise to pay a bill depending on
what money you have to collect. Have your goods
in departments, infants', children's, misses', ladies',
boys', men's, etc., grades and prices as systematically
and convenient as the size of your store will allow.
If you are a practical workman and understand buying you may open a store with small capital. If you

have a knowledge of the business, but not a practical workmen, in a city of 20,000 population you might start with $3,000 or $4,000, but if you have no experience of the business, do not invest in it until you learn some knowledge of it. Be honest in your dealings, gentlemanly in your manners, attentive to your business with a liking for it, and you will make it successful."

As I arose to leave, he concluded by saying : " By the way, Mr.——told me you were going in the business."

"Yes, in M——, about eighteen miles from here."

"Well, I wish you success, and anything I can do for you I will be only too happy."

"Good-by." And to my readers I wish the same.

How to Manage a Retail Shoe Store.

BY MRS. RUTH BOND, BRILLIANT, OHIO.

I have been reading, with great interest, the letters from different and prominent retail shoe dealers, published in the BOOT AND SHOE RECORDER, on "How to Manage a Retail Shoe Store," and although not entitled personally to be a contestant, according to 4th and 5th terms, viz., "All contributors must be subscribers to the RECORDER," "No one to enter the contest unless he is a retail shoe dealer, and now in business," yet being my husband's helpmeet and chief clerk and manager of store during his absence, I feel, as he is included in both 4th and 5th terms, that I would like to say a few words in a simple manner, remembering throughout this letter that I am not an advocate of women's rights only so far as equal re-muneration for equal service is just, equitable and right. In this connection I wish to be considered as a pupil, eager to learn from the experience and sug-gestions of those who have won their knowledge of the shoe business in all its grand details, by hard-earned and hard-won labor and experience.

"No excellence without great labor," was one of childhood's maxims, ever written in our old-time copy books as models. With this thought I desire your careful consideration. The beautifully moulded vase with its lines of figures of exquisite grace and loveliness must be hardened in the fiery furnace, so must all our faculties be developed by use, hardened and strengthened by experience, matured by cheerful and honest discharge of our duties in whatever sphere we are placed. He is a wise man who knows how to employ the means and energies of this mighty age. Hence the first requisite to successfully manage a retail shoe store would be experience ; for I believe, to be systematically arranged and successfully managed, it is an art. 2d. Capital sufficient to buy our first stock for cash, followed, if possible, by a complete cash system, thus saving expense of book-keeper in a great degree, which will enable us to give our customers the benefit of our purchases, curtailing expenses in all things, as this comes in room of capital. 3d. Location, which selection depends chiefly upon capital and the class of trade from whom you expect your chief patronage. If capital is small or moderate, let your surroundings be neat, tasteful and cleanly, colors harmonizing or contrasting, as desired. If capital large, and the desire to cater "to the best trade only" be your object, then select a handsome room in a fashionable business location. Have all the latest styles in colorings, in fine high-priced shoes and boots, changing frescoings, brass fixtures, hassocks, umbrella stands, cuspidores, etc., cushioned settees, center-table, floor-mats (the last should be used by plain as well as stylish dealers, thus placing cus-

tomers on their guard against soiling bottom of shoes).
Walnut and oak are pretty combinations when well
arranged, giving the necessary dark and light shades.
In winter have bottom of windows covered with red,
either woolens, velveteen, velvet or whatever is in line
with circumstances and surroundings. In summer
place some cream-colored open goods over red covering, to give a cool, airy effect. Arrange shoes neatly,
tastefully, changing styles, etc., to suit the season.

Now we come to the rules and suggestions that
will apply universally. A dealer should be the possessor of good judgment and the art of using it, good
knowledge of human nature, and discernment of customers' taste, as indicated by dress and actions.
Each department to itself, embracing all grades,
ladies' first, commencing with finer grades, placed in
single cartons, one above another, arranged in
sizes running from right to left, or left to right, as the
case may be. Nos. 2½ one above another, 3 and
3½, etc., with each width, as such, A, B, C, D and E,
in line, labeled and marked on end of carton. Misses'
department, second, embracing all grades same as
ladies'. Children's next, and child's and infants' arranged in similar manner. Men's department, boys'
and youths' 5 and 6 widths arranged same way on
other side of the room. Boots boxed and under
cover, plainly numbered on bottom as follows : 6-36,
7-36, 8-36, 9-36, etc., with mate same. Boys', youths'
and child's marked the same way. Rubber goods in
rubber department alone, and in the coolest part of
the room. Room considerably longer than wide, if

possible; for instance, length, 60 feet; width, 20
feet; height, 16 feet, etc.

Buy from well-known manufacturers and jobbers,
such goods, and only such, as your trade and the
times demand, selecting not too many kinds, but
keeping up sizes in all departments. Be not ready to
condemn a whole line. It occasionally we find a pair
that does not give entire satisfaction, remember the
old saying, "When you find a friend that is good
and true, don't change the old one for the new."
Take account of every sale, profit and item of expense, so that at a moment's notice you can tell exactly
your financial standing.

Let a shoe be just as represented. Take pleasure
in showing customers different grades of goods and
any particular nice line you may have, even if not
asked for, as by doing so you often effect sales.
Teach them to distinguish the difference in stock,
such as pebble goat from grain, showing that one is
but an imitation of the other. Let them see that you
consider their interests and yours are identical. Gain
their confidence by giving them the value of their
money, and should an article guaran·eed by you prove
worthless, make amends by a liberal reduction on the
next pair. Be not afraid of overpleasing by courtesies,
kind and attentive manners. To ladies, particularly,
speak of their nicely proportioned feet, and say how
beautifully they fit, what a pretty instep, etc. We are
all susceptible to flattery (I mean the ladies). Men
take matters more philosophically. We have been
using a nice line of hosiery in the medium and fash-

ionable shades, black and dark hues, some bright
shades (only a few), for as Mr. Arnold says, "We
must try to please the multitude." Often by having
nice dry hose to offer to ladies at a low figure, we can
sell them shoes that would not otherwise go on so
easily or fit nicely when the hose were wet with per-
spiration. In order that they may have some seclu-
sion, have a nice little nook neatly carpeted and hid-
den by a screen, where they may try on shoes. Wash-
bowl, towel, soap, combs and brush, mirror, etc.,
would be quite an addition, so that she can re-adjust
hair and toilet. They make a great impression of home
attractiveness. Much trouble might be avoided in
taking out goods on approval if we have a neat, cosy
apartment as suggested above.

Don't always give a customer size asked for, for if
we do, we are sure to have a great many damaged
shoes, such as button-holes, nicely worked ones, too,
broken, sometimes counters broken down and the
shoe is condemned instantly as of no account, when
it has been stamped out of existence. Manufacturers
are often censured by retailers when it is no fault of
stock, workmanship or anything, but trying to crowd
a foot into a shoe that is entirely too small to admit
of it, much less bear the pressure of the entire body
to which it is subjected. Better miss a sale than sell a
shoe one or more sizes too small, for customers, as a
rule, are selfish enough to look to their own interest
without considering your discomfiture, time or loss.

Certain causes produce certain results, and a successful manager brings all these items to bear in the

management of his business. Life is made up of small items. Within themselves they amount to little, but in the aggregate produce lasting and great results. Much depends on the shape of a shoe, its proportions, outlines, etc., the manner of presenting it to a customer, etc. Always rebutton shoes before replacing in cartons, as they retain their shape so much better when buttoned. All these are some of the many little things, but of great importance in effecting sales.

We have so far forgotten the security of insurance and the necessity of judicious advertising. By all means keep your stock well insured in safe and reliable companies.

Lastly, but not least, let me kindly admonish you all not to forget to read weekly and carefully, the BOOT AND SHOE RECORDER, for by so doing we can educate ourselves and obtain fresh, new and valuable knowledge to assist us in properly managing a retail boot and shoe store.

Thanking the kind managers of the same for the knowledge we have derived from them in the past, and for the high privilege extended us for the exchange of ideas in thus promoting our best interests through this medium, and anxiously awaiting the next letter on "How to Manage a Retail Boot and Shoe Store," I will close this article, feeling that it is partial return for what I have learned from the others.

How to Manage a Retail Shoe Store.

BY JAMES S. CAMPBELL, WEST NEWTON, MASS.

I will give you my experience in retailing shoes. As a convenient and well-arranged store is desirable, I will commence with fitting up a store. About ten years ago I hired a store in a new block and had it fitted up to suit me. The store that I was then using was small, the drawers were wide and shallow, and the shoes would frequently turn up if I had more than one tier in a drawer, and would likely be damaged more or less when pulling the drawers out. Rubber shoes I had to have all sizes mixed up in drawers. I thought I could remedy that and make other improvements in the new store.

The new store was about 25x50 feet. I had a partition run across far enough from the back of the store to make a good back shop. On the front of the partition I had shelves put up and had them divided into pigeon holes of sufficient size and number to hold a few pairs of ladies' and gentlemen's rubber overshoes of each size and width. I found them very convenient and a great saving over the old way of pulling over a drawerful, and then perhaps not finding what I wanted. Lengthwise of the front shop

(87)

I had three tiers of drawers on each side and shelves above them, the highest of which was within easy reach standing on the floor, thus doing away with the necessity of pulling out a drawer or having a ladder to stand on. The cover over the drawers projected out from the shelves wide enough to be used instead of a counter. The only counter I had was a short one in front of the rubber shelves, for wrapping paper, peg cutters, iron lasts, etc.

Instead of show cases I had about one-half of the shelving on one side of the store covered with glass doors in which I could show shoes that I did not want to put in the windows, and, as I had no counters in the way, the customers could look at them, and they would frequently see a shoe they wanted. I had two large plate glass show windows, one each side the door. In regard to the drawers I will say that the dimensions inside were about eight inches deep, seventeen inches wide, and thirty inches long, with one handle in the middle to pull the drawers out with, and these were made so as to pull out very easily. I had enough of them, so that I was not obliged to put three or four sizes in one drawer, thus avoiding the necessity of pulling over a drawful of shoes to find the size I wanted. I had a heavy moulding put on the top of the shelves and partition which added much to the appearance of the store, and the cover to the top shelf could be used for empty cartons. I had four settees about twelve feet long each, two on each side of the store, with a wide passage way between them. The settees were covered with heavy carpeting and were about fourteen inches high without backs. I had a strip of carpet laid on the floor loosely between the drawers and settees.

Now, in regard to the amount of stock a retailer should have in his store and the quality of his goods, it depends ent'rely upon his location and the class of people he expects to sell to, the capital he has to invest and the distance his store is from the base of his supplies. When a retailer has filled up his store with regular sizes of cases, it is better as he sells to fill up sizes than to order regular cases, and any retailer who does persist in ordering regular sizes will find when he takes account of stock that he has a lot of sizes that were not called for, and they will soon be shopworn goods. I contend that if a buyer understands his business, and his clerks do their duty, he will have very few damaged or shopworn goods. When a customer has tried on a pair of shoes and they did not fit, they should be put back in their place before another pair is tried on, instead of throwng them on the counter till the customer goes; and when another customer comes who wants that size and quality, try that pair instead of a fresh pair. It is not necessary to let a customer try on many pairs to get a fit. An observant clerk can tell by the looks of the customer's foot and shoe very near the size that is wanted, and if the first pair does not fit, the second pair should, if the retailer has plenty of widths of the kind wanted.

Now, in regard to altering buttons, which has become to be almost a nuisance in some stores, if they do not have a lightning button fastener. Frequently, when trying on ladies' boots, they will say they fit just splendidly over the ball but are a little tight over the instep, and if you will alter the buttons a little they will be all right, but instead of that I give her a size wider and they are pretty sure to fit her.

A great many rubber overshoes are spoiled by trying on. A lady, for instance, asks for a No. 4 overshoe ; you try them but can't get them on, and 4½ with the same result ; but No. 5 goes on but it is too wide or too narrow. Now to remedy that I always have a size stick handy, and I never try on a rubber over-shoe till I have measured the length of the shoe. If it is a lady that wants a pair and her shoe measures No. 5 on the outside, I should give her a No. 5 over-shoe, and if the boot was wide and thick-soled, give her a wide rubber, but if medium width and thin sole, give her a medium rubber, and in nine cases out of ten the first pair will fit.

My experience in retailing boots and shoes has been mostly with medium-priced goods, and I have sold the same make of some kinds for more than ten years, and the quality is the same all the time. I make it a point to keep plenty of widths of each kind, and then it is a pleasure to fit a customer. I think it is for the interest of the retailer when he gets hold of a good shoe to stick to it, whether he buys it of the manufacturer or jobber or drummer, as long as it proves good. A retailer who is a good judge of stock and knows how a shoe is made has

an advantage in buying over the retailer who knows
little or nothing about stock, or less about making.
If a retailer buys his shoes of drummers they soon
find out whether he is a good judge of shoes or not,
and if not he is the customer that the drummer, if
inclined to be tricky, will sell shoes that are not just
what they should be.

Now, in regard to putting shoes in the window to
show. To let them stay week after week with the sun
shining on them, as some do is entirely wrong. They
should be changed as often as once a week, and the
sun should not be allowed to shine on them. One
of those very warm days recently, I was passing
by a shoe store where the shoes in the window were
exposed to the full rays of the burning sun, and the
oil was actually oozing out of the leather, and of
course those shoes were nearly spoiled. They probably would be sold to some customer who would be
likely to bring them back in a few days with the uppers burst where they had been scorched by the sun,
and the blame will be put on the manufacturer for
putting in poor leather. Light and dust injures all
shoes more or less ; the fine sharp dust works into
the pores of the leather and is frequently the cause of
the uppers cracking. All fine calf shoes, unless in
single cartons, should be wrapped up in pairs in strong
paper with the size and width plainly marked on the
outside. I do not think as favorably of cartons as I
did when thay first came round. I thought by keeping each pair single, the retailer would always have
his goods clean and in good shape, but I soon found

that the average clerk, and, in fact, the retailer himself, would seldom put the shoes back in the carton
in good shape, and I have seen many a pair of ladies'
fine kid boot uppers wrinkled and crumpled and
nearly spoiled by being taken out and put.back with a
jam, without regard to how they were put in when
new. Some cartons are too small for the shoes that
are crowded into them, and it would take an expert
packer to put some of them back in shape after they
have been tried on a few times. I have thought a
good many times when I have taken a pair of shoes
out of the carton with the uppers all crumpled up,
that it would be better for the retailer if the manufacturer would put the cost of the carton in the shoe
or make a discount to the buyer, and not put his
shoes in cartons. I think it would be a good idea to
have the carton business brought before the Retail
Dealers' Association, and get the experience of the
retailers in different parts of the country.

I think a great many retailers make a mistake by
putting in too many kinds of shoes, especially of the
high cost and fancy kinds. It is better to lose the
sale of a pair occasionally, than to put in such goods.
I do not refer, of course, to the large fashionable
stores in cities, that carry from $10,000 to $30,000
in stock, and a trade to correspond with such a capital, as they must keep such goods, and there is where
people will go who want such shoes. If a customer
wants you to get a pair for him, you can get them at
such stores, and they will usually divide the profits
with you.

Shoes that have been kept on hand some time will naturally have a slightly shop-worn appearance ; but a little neats-foot oil rubbed on the uppers will make them pliable, and look as fresh as new. For coarse uppers, such as calf, kip or split a thick dressing, such as is kept by most finding stores, is the best thing I know of, but, if that cannot be had, gum tragacanth dissolved thin and a little ink put in, or thin paste will do after oiling the shoes.

Smoothing the bottoms of shoes after they get badly scratched, has given me more trouble in trying to make them look new, and given me less satisfaction than any other part of the shoe. Some bottoms can be scraped and sand-papered, and will look well ; while others will look better by wetting down with water or oxalic acid. When any or all of these ways make them look worse, it is better to black the bottoms all over, rub down when not quite dry, and go over the bottoms with a coat or two of any ladies' boot dressing.

I don't know as I can say anything that would be useful to any retailer about how he should use his customers. I look upon it as a purely business matter. I have the shoes to sell, and it is for my interest to use the customer well. I am in favor of and always have sold on the one-price system to all. Goods should be sold at a fair profit, say 25 per cent above cost on an average, and for just what they are. If you misrepresent your goods, people will soon find it out, and will be pretty sure to leave you and advise their friends to do the same, so that in a short time you will find your trade growing beautifully less.

If the business of a retailer is such as to require him to employ two or more clerks, he should see that they handle the shoes carefully, and put them back in their places neatly. If you have a clerk who will not do it, discharge him at once, and the clerks will soon learn that they must be neat and careful if they want to stay with you. It is important, also, that the retailer himself should be as particular as he wants his clerks to be, and if he sees his shoes in the window, day after day, with the sun shining on them, and does not have them covered from the sun, he must not expect the clerks will do it when he is away.

In regard to advertising, I think that when the trade is strictly local it is of little use to advertise unless you have something new to which you wish to draw attention ; then get up a neat card with a pretty picture on it, that the children will take home to keep. Common circulars are not worth the paper they are printed on ; but if you have through trade, or trade from neighboring towns, it is a good idea to let those people know what you have to sell if you want their trade.

Mr. Editor, I have given above my experience in the retail boot and shoe business. If it is what you want, use it ; if not, cremate it.

How to Manage a Retail Shoe Store.

BY M. L. WILSON, ATTICA, IND.

I thought I would tell you what I know about "How to Manage a Retail Shoe Store." I may strike an overlooked point. I am forty-five years old, have been in the shoe business fourteen years. Am learning something about it every week.

I do not expect to describe a palace like the "Day-Sewed" people have, but a country shoe store. In the first place get the best location you can. It will cost more, but will be worth more to you in the end. Give your store a name different from the firm name. People locate it in their minds better. I call my store the "Blue Front Shoe Store." After you select the name never change it. Mine is painted blue on outside from top to bottom, with my name in gilt across the front. My wooden signs are all painted blue with white letters. They should be large, and set at intervals on every road to your town as far out as you reach trade, even if it is fifteen or twenty miles. I make it a rule to have my wrapping paper printed in blue ink, also use blue envelopes with letter-heads and statements in blue print. I have a blue label, and paste it on the top of every individual carton. This I consider a good advertisement.

1 write all my own advertisements for the local papers, and change them every two weeks. I have a regular space in the paper, and never allow the editor to shift it around. I have a number of cuts I use at the top of my "advertisement." Then I generally have reading matter with a brief reference to my business. This way you are sure to have your advertisement read every week. This is my last advertisement :

"Josh Billings says, ' With all your getting get knowledge.' Solomon says, ' Get understanding.' Leaving you to decide which you prefer, we would add that there are plenty of places to obtain the former if you have plenty of money ; but if you are short of cash there is only one place to obtain the latter, and that is the ' Blue Front Shoe Store.' "

I have the show windows washed and dressed every Monday morning. I use red flannel for floor of window. You can design structures of various kinds in the window with empty cartons. Cover them with red oil calico. The contrast shows the shoes effectively. Have the interior shelved for individual cartons, with a base about two feet wide at bottom of shelves, a row of large drawers under. This is very convenient. These can be left open in daytime with two or three samples hanging out of each one. From the top of the shelves to ceiling on each side I have a nice lot of empty cartons arranged systematically, so as to appear as if they were surplus goods. It makes a nice show. Often customers remark, " What an amount of goods you sell from the immense stock you carry." I have ladies', misses' and children's on one side, men's, boys' and youths' on the other. I use no counters. I have three tables in center of room, one under each chandelier, to wrap goods on, with spaces between covered with nice pattern of Brussells and there we try on shoes. This makes it handy from either side and saves running around counters. A show case on each side in front can be used to good advantage. The office desk in the rear, with plenty of light, pictures on the wall, a few nice plants, good bloomers, and an English ivy, that is green all winter can be trailed with good effect, makes the rear look neat and cheerful.

Retain your customers when they come to trade as long as you can, and get familiar with them. Cover all the goods at night, and wipe all exposed goods every morning with flannel cloth ; this saves knocking dust all around with duster. Treat old folks and children as pleasant as you do the belles and dudes. Always open and shut door after your customers, and invite them back. This takes a little more time, but it pays. They conclude you have more than a money interest in them. Supply customers with just what they want. Never dictate nor insist they shall take something else.

I take measures for all irregular feet. I have a list of twenty lady customers who wear from thirteens to number nines for whom I get fine shoes made ; this feature pays me well. If you fit a lady that has a bad foot, she will advertise largely for you, and you

are sure to sell her friends. Never allow a clerk or
employe to discuss the topics of the day in the store
with a customer. Always talk something germane
to the business. Once or twice during the
year write a personal letter to each of your
customers, calling attention to anything new that
you have in stock, and invite them in to see it; this
way you keep well acquainted with your trade.
You cannot get a customer into your store too often.
One feature of the shoe business is, that the visits
are not frequent enough. We forget some of our
trade.

Keep a drawer for all your soiled and undesirable
odds and ends, and when you have a customer for
cheap shoes go to that drawer. You will be surprised to see how clean you can keep your stock if
this is attended to. I keep all the old stock I have
in one drawer, and sometimes it is nearly empty.
Never set one pair of shoes out to customers and then
stare at them till they decide, but show them a variety
of shoes and give them liberty in selecting, and never
leave a customer to wait on some one else. It won't
pay if you intend to stay in the business.

It you are situated where you are called on frequently by travelers, buy goods often and have them
coming in every week. They sell better when they
are fresh. The facilities for getting goods now don't
justify a man in loading up at one time for the season. I never go to market. I can buy better of the
agents, and save time and money. Never buy what
you do not want, nor more than you want. " Drive

a stake " here on this, no matter how plausible the drummer, then you will never be "loaded." When cases come in take the lid off, turn it up and nail it on bottom, it is then out of the way and ready for use. I mark all goods with cost and selling price on bottom, also size and mate number. I have no mismates in stock.

As to clerks, if the proprietor is industrious and energetic, his clerks will soon imbibe his spirit. You all know this is a fact ; like begets like. A lazy indolent dealer would soon ruin any good clerk.

If shoemen are alive, dry goods houses cannot handle shoes in small places successfully. The peculiarties connected with a shoe store they cannot indulge in. For instance, manufacturing and repairing ; they cannot sew rips, paste on patches, and tend to the little details like a shoeman. If you don't mend and make for them, they will go where they can get it done, and they will likely buy there, too. The shoemen of our place have an association five years old. We meet every once in a while. Keep on good terms with each other, talk the business over, weed out the evils, keep a black list and compare it all around. We avoid cutting prices ; we sell rubbers at a profit, and in fact our relations are mutual. We work together. Keep well insured ; this strengthens your credit if you need it. If not it fills your pocket if you have a fire. Never tell customers you are selling them a shoe at cost, even if you do (unless it is out of your old drawer), they won't think as much of you if you do. People naturally like to boost a man up hill if he is going that way, and kick him down if he has started. Sell as near for cash as you can. Never trust a doubtful customer; learn to say "No" firmly, but courteously.

Avoid inviting loafers to your store. Always return the money for shoes if customer is not suited. Attend to all the little details gratuitously; fasten on a button, take off a heel lift, supply a lace; by doing this cheerfully you win your way into the affections of your trade. Don't "boss" your clerks in the presence of customers. Address them as Mr. Smith, Mr. Brown, etc. Never talk loud in the store. Be truthful and get the confidence of your customer. Be honest, cheerful, and my word for it you will succeed.

How to Manage a Retail Shoe Store.

BY G. D. SIMEN, ALLEGHENY, PA.

Having read all the articles in your valuable paper on "How to Manage a Retail Boot and Shoe Store," I will try and give my ideas and points on it too.

Among the first qualities, to be successful in a retail boot and shoe store, and as I have grown up in a shoe store from the bench, and succeeded well, would say first of all never have a boot or shoe or try to sell one, unless you are positive that your customer gets full value in buying the goods, no matter if the shoes only cost 25 cents a pair. This must be the aim and convicton to start with, and success will crown every honest effort.

In order to classify the different kinds of retail boot and shoe stores, I put them down as No. 1, No. 2, No. 3, and I like to bluff off some of the drummers trying to sell poor or extremely fine goods by naming them Buttermilk, Milk and Cream.

No. 1, Buttermilk, I call all shoddy and poor auction goods ; No. 2, Milk, all good solid leather goods well-made and reliable ; No. 3, Cream, all extras, extra fine in style and price. These are the three kinds of stores, and you will find them in all large cities. In smaller towns the No. 2 is the best, and will succeed. Neither No. 1 or No. 3 has enough custom to maintain itself.

Now, my advice to all is, be careful and know where you start. If in a large city, ask yourself in which No. 1, No. 2, or No. 3, you are most suitable for, and if you want to do a large bnsiness go for No. 2. Keep plenty of good "Milk," good regular goods, at prices that are popular, and you will see by each day's sales what your customers want, and can pay for. Be sure and be on the lookout for the best goods at the lowest prices. Give your customers a good selection both in style and quality, so they know when they come and buy that you want to do them good. Have them well suited both in comfort and quality of goods.

Now, in order to do a large business, say $50,000 to $100,000 per annum, and all for cash, no credit, you must use all your ability and judgment, and have plenty of goods at prices to suit, and still not so many as to accumulate old stock. Have as near as possible what your customers want and can pay for. Study all the wants of your customers well. Be careful to avoid all or most all extras ; that is, you will see new styles and new goods coming every season, something new every sesaon, some extra high and some extra low cut, some narrow and some broad. Look at them and see if your customers will be bene-fitted by the change. Mind ! you are working for the people ; they will have to buy your goods. Be-sides, you will get so many more new styles and kinds, that before you look around you have too many extras on hand, and are short on your old reliable, good every-day sellers, so you will have to force your extras out at a loss. Force no new styles on your customers as long as they are satisfied with your regular goods. To illustrate just one kind : You have a very good line of children's and misses' shoes, they are high enough cut, look well, sell well and wear well. The drummer comes along and says : "Here is something new that takes well. Mr. So-and-So sells lots of them. You see they are extra high, something new." I see they are very nice, and no doubt could use them, but see here, my drummer, the children's I sell sizes 8 to 11 at $1 ; the misses', 12 to 2, at $1.25. Now, your extra high 8 to 12 at $1, and 13 to 2 at $1.25, I would have to sell at $1.25 and $1.50, and how much would my customer be benefited for the extra 25 cents per pair? Only one button higher, by paying the extra 25 cents per pair ! The benefit would be none at all. If I do not charge more I am at a loss. More styles, more goods, and no benefit whatever to my customers.

Keep clear of almost all the extras, where you or your customers are not benefited by the change. If a new style comes out, and it takes well, all right. Do not be the first to force it on the market. Let others do it. If you have calls for them order a small lot of medium-priced, and if they sell well you know what to do. In all my dealings I try to have goods that sell themselves, have them in style, quality and price, so they meet with a ready sale and are wanted. Keep and always have plenty of the good

regular salable goods and you will not lose many sales.
Now, in regard to the different kinds. Always
keep children's and misses' shoes of a very good
quality, and sell them at a very small profit, because
children and misses, boys and youths are your best
customers. They wear out more shoes, 5 to 1,
against the parents. Give them good goods that will
wear, or none at all. If you sell the children good
shoes, you will sell the parents also. So be careful,
and keep the right kind.

As for ladies, you can keep some cheap goods, especially for old ladies, and still be good. For instance, you can buy a good lasting congress at 60
cents per pair and 6 off, and sell it for 75 cents,
much to your customer's satisfaction. Also a lasting
slipper at 40 cents and sell it for 50 cents. Sell
them, if possible, better grades at $1 to $1.50.

In leather goods keep none so cheap. Be careful
that every customer gets his money's worth in the
goods bought. You must know, and your salesman,
too, the different wants of your customers.

You are selling to the city girl, the city lady, the
mother, and your country customer; they all want
different shoes and prices to suit. The city girl will
want a cheap, stylish shoe ; the city lady will pay any
price, so you suit her; the mother will want comfort ; and your country customer will not be very
particular, so they wear well and are medium-priced.
In men's shoes it is the same difference. Have shoes
that will please the eye and fit the feet, and wear well,
at the right price. Give them all as good shoes as

they can afford to pay for, and you will soon find out what kinds and prices take and sell best. Mind your own business, do not imitate others, but see the kind of customers you have, and supply their wants well and fully.

To sum up the whole question how to manage a retail shoe store and succeed well:

First of all have a practical good experience, if possible brought up f om the bench.

Second, get the best plac: in town for your store.

Third, study the wants of your customers, so you will have the right kind of goods at popular prices, and that every pair will give full value for the money paid for them.

Fourth, avoid all extras in two many new styles, and keep plenty of good, regular, salable goods that sell themselves.

Fif h. the profits to be (the smallest) say about 20 per cent on children s, misses', boys' and youths' shoes, and from 25 to 40 on ladies' and men's goods.

Sixth, to start out and buy for cash. Discount all your bills, pay prompt, and only increase your business with your profits. Your store is your bank, and all your gain is made by discount and profits.

So, among the three kinds of stores to retail boots and shoes, start with No. 2, have very little "butter-milk," except in summer for ladies' cheap shoes. Keep plenty of good fresh "milk." Ke p very little "cream," it ge s sour too quick. If you yourself are pleasant, and your salesmen too, mind your business well, have a nice clean store as attractive as possible, with goods in complete order, so you have no trouble in finding sizes and showing goods to advantage (everything can be plain and nice without being expensive), you will succeed and be happy.

This is my experience the last twenty-two years, and I am today well satisfied and happy in my calling.

How to Manage a Retail Shoe Store.

BY E. C. RICHMOND, PHILADELPHIA, PA.

The management of a retail shoe store, if judged by the number of shoe houses one meets with in a day's journey, would seem to be a trifling affair; but, judged by the standard of success, it becomes a question of some importance in the mercantile community.

The leading features to be observed in the conduct of a successful retail shoe store are location, fitting up, selection of stock, method of keeping help, etc.

Having procured a suitable store and considered the character and surroundings of your neighborhood, fit it up neatly, with a due regard to the conveniences for keeping stock, and with an eye to the comfort of customers. And in connection with this matter I would advise single pair stock boxes for regular lines of goods, as they present a neat appearance and are decidedly handy. In arranging your stock keep your lines well together and compact. Let size, width, and price be marked plainly on each box, so that salespeople may see at a glance just what you have, and thereby serve customers promptly.

In making selections for stock see that no two lines
of goods conflict, either in quality, price, or style.
Keep as few lines of shoes as possible, taking care
always that they are the popular shapes and styles,
and as few pairs of a size and width in stock boxes
as may be convenient. Draw constantly from your
reserve to keep filled up. Less goods in stock means
less shopworn shoes. Have your reserve stock in
nearly the same order as your selling stock, and fill
up from it. Keep constantly before your mind what
lines of goods are carried, and see if you can do with
one less. Fewer lines of goods means a more complete assortment of sizes in those carried and with less
stock. While on this subject I would advise retailers
to do away with the practice of placing large orders
for goods twice a year, but keep buying all the time.
Keep your reserve stock so many pairs ahead, according to the selling quality of the shoes. I find it
is an excellent plan to have the manufacturers you
are dealing with keep a certain number of salable
sizes and widths made up for you, subject to your order, and draw freely upon them. In this way sizes
can always be kept up.

Having once placed your lines of goods and prac-
tically tested them as to quality, style, fit, etc., make
as few changes as possible, and then only for cause.
Remember, nothing breaks up sizes and produces old
stock and odds and ends like frequent changing, and
nothing tends more to elevate and improve the quality
of your goods than large purchases from the same
manufacturers. They become interested, and besides

giving lowest figures will steadily improve the quality
of shoes furnished. I believe that I have had more
pressure brought to induce changes (and sometimes
by most intimate friends whom I would gladly serve)
than any man in the business ; but, having a thorough
knowledge of my regular lines, I have steadily de-
clined to make any changes, except for cause.

Do not always see how cheap goods can be bought,
but how well. By too close buying more or less injury is caused, and manufacturers are often compelled
to take the life out of the shoes in order to produce
them cheap. Pay a fair price and have the goods
just right. Customers have a great faculty for discov-
ering where good shoes are sold, and travel blocks to
find them. Let your store be one of this class.

Having fitted up your store and stocked it with
salable goods, advertise the fact and invite the public
to come and see for themselves. Be sure the shoes
are what you represent them to be. I firmly believe
in the art of advertising. Many of our most noted
men have become successful by a liberal use of
printer's ink.

One of the most important features in connection
with the management of a retail shoe store is the selection of salespeople, and too much care and attention cannot be given to this subject. I hold that
every man should, like Cuvier, the French naturalist,
thoroughly know his business. So proficient was he
in the study of natural history that you might bring
him a bone and he could tell the species of animal to
which it belonged. The whole matter is now in this

shape : A store has been leased or bought, fitted up and stocked with an assortment of salable goods. The fact has been advertised, and it now rests upon the energy and ability of the salespeople to sell the goods, and make the venture a success.

Therefore, employ the best talent, pay them well and make them feel comfortable. Remember, a careful, competent salesman will earn his salary every day upon customers whom mediocrity or indifference will allow to pass out with scarcely an effort. I have frequently observed good customers leave stores not suited, when, by a little judicious management, sales might have been effected. One reason given for losing sales is, that the goods asked for are not kept in stock.

Now, no store can afford to keep every kind of shoes asked for by peculiar or curious customers. Your true salesman, who has a thorough knowledge of all the makes that have been in the market for the past five or six years, will inform those particular people that such goods are entirely out of the market, or are not suited to the present condition of affairs, at the same time producing something that will fill the bill. I have seen this tried, and as a result sales were affected again and again. Of course there are times when customers will insist upon having precisely what they ask for, and will take nothing else, and we are reluctantly compelled to allow them to go ; but I have seen some of the most positive kind of people leave the store perfectly satisfied with an entirely different kind of shoe than first asked for, and have known them to return again for the same goods. It is not always what people ask for, but rather what they ought to have. A good fit often produces a splendid sale and makes you a customer for all time to come.

If there are two or more salespeople in your store, or, if you have but one in connection with yourself, try the experiment of referring customers from one to another. Dozens of sales are made by a judicious reference, and very often the customer will purchase the same shoe from the second person that he refused from the first. Do not imagine because you, the proprietor, fail to make sales that they cannot be made, try the process of referring them to your faithful clerk, and you will often be surprised at the result. I speak from a personal knowledge, and know the value of this. I have in my department today a man who earns double his salary every week upon referred customers alone.

One of the greatest evils of the shoe business is improper fitting. The majority of people will, if not advised and reasoned with, wear their shoes too short, and here is where your competent salesman again comes to the front; and by a fine tact and perseverance succeeds in properly fitting the customer; and shoes fitted properly will wear longer, and look better, besides being more comforable to the wearer. Can we expect all these qualities from incompetent, poorly paid, or indifferent salespeople? Is it not much better to get the best and pay for it rather than have your business fail through incompetent people?

I consider the question of proper fitting, in connection with the management of a retail shoe store, a most important one. One of the first principles laid down by me in my present management was, that no matter what else might occur, customers must be fitted. I have insisted upon having this principle carried out, and when customers (as they will at times do) take a poor fitting or short shoe, they are told before they leave the department that the shoes do not fit properly. I believe that this is one of the reasons why the great house of John Wanamaker has so firmly retained so much of its shoe business year after year.

Finally, have customers waited upon promptly upon entering the store. Anticipate their wants, and when the sale is finished dismiss them politely.

Never deceive them ; have your goods marked in plain figures, and sell upon a strictly one-price basis. Tell your customers precisely what the goods are, whether hand or machine-sewed, calfskin or buff leather. By these methods confidence is inspired and success insured.

How to Manage a Retail Shoe Store.

BY E. L. JONES, ODELL, ILL.

Secure a good location, even if you have to pay more rent than to be to one side. Make your store front attractive by painting the front with colors that are pleasing to the eye, and also attract attention. Keep the windows clean, and make a fine display of goods in them, making a change once a week or oftener if you have time. Let your clerks try their hand at trimming the windows; perhaps they may show more taste than the old man. Light up your store and show windows in good shape at night. Better to have too much light than not enough. Have a tasty sign outside and also in your show windows.

In arranging your shelving have your shelves not over four feet high with only a light cornice, and the over-head made tight, so the dust will not drop down through. It also will give you a chance to make a display of goods on top of your shelving. If you use counters in front have them made light and tasty, avoiding big heavy brackets, etc. Have your side walls and ceilings painted or papered. Over your shelving you can hang fancy signs, etc., as you see fit. Take pains in arranging your goods on the shelves.

(113)

If you use single cartons mark the price, kind, width and size on the outside of each box. For this purpose you should use fancy gummed tags, size $\frac{1}{2} \times \frac{1}{4}$, sticking them on the lower right-hand corner. For marking each pair of boots and shoes use a smaller tag, sticking it on the shank of the shoe near the heel, for nothing looks worse than big sprawling letters marked in ink or pencil on the soles of the goods, and you cannot alter them if you should wish to. On shoes, etc., when the sizes are not already marked, mark sizes with pencil on the heel next to the shank of the shoe; you can do that as easily as to mark them on the sole. Mark your sizes in this way: 30 for No. 3; 32 for 3½, and so on. Ninety out of every hundred women wear shoes too small for them. Don't contradict a woman when she says she used to wear size four—and fives are a snug fit now—perhaps she did, but it was years ago. The manufacturers will mark the size on the inside as you want them. In that way you can fit every person and give shoes that will cause better satisfaction. If you happen to be out of a certain size called for, fit the person with a half size larger, and he or she will be none the wiser.

Don't buy your goods of every Tom and Dick that comes along; confine yourself to as few houses as possible, and stick to the line of goods that gives your trade the best satisfaction. The reasons for buying of few houses are many. In the first place you are not so apt to accumulate odds and ends; then again, you can always sort up on sizes, and if you in-

sist on their only selling you in the town, they will do
it. Any house or salesman will tell you he would
rather have one good customer in each place that he
can rely on, than to take his chances with all the other
house in the country. Good reliable manufacturers
will not take the advantage of you ; competition is too
strong in these times.

Post yourself on what goes into a boot or shoe, the
prices of labor in making, etc. Half of the retail
dealers don't know the value of a boot or shoe, the
cost of making, the cost of stock, etc., and it is very
necessary that they should. Solid sole leather inner
soles and counters always give better satisfaction than
shoddy ones. Don't sell cheap goods if you can
avoid it. If you have to, tell the parties buying what
they may expect, and if they still think they are getting a gold mine, it is their own fault, not yours.

Sell goods for cash. Study up something new in
the way of advertising. Don't copy after some of
your neighbors. Keep your name and business before the people ; let them know you sell good goods,
and back them up as recommended.

Keep a record of sales each day, the cost and
amount received. Each night figure up cost and
amount received, and you have your profit. Enter
this each day in a book for that purpose ; have this
book ruled in three columns, one for the amount sold,
the second for the cost, and the third for the profits ;
also have the month and year written at the top of
the page. At the end of the month figure them up.
After you have practiced this a year you will not do

without it. It is a separate thing from your cash book.

In wrapping up goods use a light Manila paper with your advertisement printed thereon. For heavy goods use a cheap grade printed paper. Do your bundles up tastily; you can do it as easily as to do them up in slipshod manner. Printed wrapping paper has many advantages over plain paper. If a person leaves a package in some other store whilst trading, nine times out of ten it will be returned to you, and you can return it to the owner.

The best of buyers will sometimes err in buying. When you have, and are stuck that way, put a price on these goods that will sell them. The longer they are in your store the harder it will be to dispose of them. Give your clerk a premium on every sale made on such goods.

Show particular attention to elderly people and children. Make your customers feel at home when they visit your place of business, showing them that you want their friendship, good-will and influence, and that you are not working purely for the mighty dollar. Never misrepresent an article; it is as easy for a merchant to tell the truth as for any other person on earth. When you have the confidence of your customers you have their trade and you will hold it, and your sales will increase each year.

Don't make your store a loafing place for every idler in town. When you meet a laboring man on the street speak to him as soon as you would to your banker. Strive to please your customers. Be at your place of business even if it is a dull day, you can always find plenty to do if you have the disposition to do it. Let each clerk have a department to keep in order. Consult with them in buying goods, you are not too old to get good ideas from them. Prompt payment of your bills when due keeps your credit good.

Don't be afraid of a little competition. Be up and doing, and success will surely crown your efforts.

How to Manage a Retail Shoe Store.

BY CLARENCE SKINNER, TOPEKA, KAS.

The establishment of this " exchange " of practical thoughts and suggestions by practical men is one of the brightest thoughts of the season, and will doubtless meet with the approval of all readers of your paper. I have been inclined to write "a few lines" on the " Management of a Retail Shoe Store."

It is needless to say there are nearly as many plans and systems in operation as there are shoe stores in the country, for every merchant who has a genuine love for his business has some ideal in his mind to which he strives to attain. Still there are general rules which might govern all to a greater or less degree. This subject taken as a whole is so broad and comprehensive it may not be possible to more than touch a few of the principal subjects. Perhaps the most important of these may be included under four heads, viz. : buying, arranging of stock, judicious advertising and selling.

The first seems an easy task to the one initiated, but to select and keep in stock the proportionate quantities of such sizes, widths and styles of shoes as are needed in the particular locality requires much forethought, calculation and judgment.

There is an old business adage which runs thus:

(118)

"Goods well bought are half sold," but a modern and more practical watchword for the merchant to place at the head of his order book is, "Buy for a Price." This does not mean buy the lowest priced goods in the market. No! No! No! On the contrary, select the very best quality, style and finish you can possibly secure to retail for a given price, which should be determined upon when the order is given, and carefully adhered to thereafter "if they are up to sample."

Make it a rule to keep posted on the whole leather and rubber market by taking as many periodicals relating to the shoe interests as can be read. Daily and weekly papers fresh from trade centers full of advertisements of "live" manufacturers are the best instructors, just as the current news of the day is of importance to the salesman.

It is well to kindly inspect the samples shown by the traveling salesmen, even though "nothing is needed now," and you are "extremely busy." It will improve your knowledge of the market, please the boys, and perhaps lead to an acquaintance of mutual profit. If an article is offered which has better style, finer finish, or appears of superior quality to that on hand of similar grade, make a minute description of it in a classified memorandum under different heads, as "Boots," "Slippers," "Women's Buttons," etc., together with manufacturer's address. This will greatly assist one with a defective memory to compare samples on the counter with those shown a month previous. Purchases may be classified in the same way by "posting" directly from the "duplicate."

Supposing now that the goods have been well-bought, their systematic arrangement is a matter of vital importance both for appearance sake and to enable the salesman the more quickly to find the desired article, and close the trade to the best advantage. Some general plan should be observed throughout the store, or at least in each department which will enable a new clerk the more quickly to learn the stock, and new goods will the more readily find the " niche " for which they were purchased. The plan very generally adopted at present by the larger shoe houses (and one equally useful in the conntry stores) is to number from the bottom upwards, and letter from left to right. Suppose the furniture is of the style usually found in shoe stores, a case of drawers supporting a broad bare shelf, with six or seven narrower ones above, about nine inches apart. The accompanying diagram will more readily illustrate the idea :

	$6.00.						$5.00.		
	A	B	C	D	E		A	B	C
8						8			
7						7			
6½						6½			
6						6			
5½						5½			
5						5			
4½				4½		4½			
4						4			
3½						3½			
3						3			
2½						2½			
2						2			

Begin at the left or front, with the finest ladies' shoe kept in stock ; place No. 2 and 2½ of the narrowest width, A, for instance, on the lower shelf ; 3 and 3½ on the next ; 4, 5, 6, 7 and 8 in consecutive order above. Let B, C, D and E follow in alphabetical order, with the same arrangement of sizes. This assigns a place for the 4½ D French kid button $6 shoe, which no other should ever occupy, even though there were sixteen pairs of 4 D and none of the right size in surplus stock above. Indicate this absehce by reversing the carton or some other convenient manner, and order at the earliest opportunity.

The next lowest-priced kid button finds a place one step farther from the front. When the kids are all placed begin with the best goat button. Then congress and front lace, each graded for quality and sized as above throughout the entire woman's department. With this classification of styles it will be found much easier to buy for a price and keep down the odds and ends. The above applies only to cartoned goods.

A sample case can be prepared for men's and boys' heavy shoes by running fixed vertical partitions through the same fixtures above referred to, so as to make six "pigeonholes," about twelve inches square, and one above the other, capable of holding two or three pairs each. Let the lower space in the front section contain all 6's of the highest-priced shoe, 7's on the next space and 11's at the top.

Now, suppose there are no $1.25 plow shoes in 8's, it is discovered when going the regular sizing rounds, and that space supplied with a significant card or empty box (never with another shoe). Why? When the next farmer customer calls for a No. 8 work shoe, the salesman will not show that style, as he sees the "blank" before showing a single shoe. In this connection another labor-saving institution, lately invented, might properly be mentioned, which is as great a luxury as the "Revolving Boot Case," mentioned in the RECORDER a few weeks ago. In most places the drawers are great rambling, roomy receptacles for everything, and that most needed oftener at the bottom than top. The improvement makes them particularly adaped for slippers, low shoes and rubbers, not in cartons. To make one, measure the length and depth of the drawers inside, cut strips of heavy tin as wide and two inches longer, double one side down, or have the tinner finish it with wire. Turn up the opposite side and each end one inch, by the aid of which you can nail the partitions securely, every $4\frac{1}{2}$ inches apart, and cross partition with inch blocks. This will give, if the drawers are from 20 to 25 inches from front to back, five spaces; each will hold four pairs of serge 50 cent buckskins, 3's in front, 4's next, etc. Then, when the fall rains and wintry blasts begin to get in their work, pack up the remaining 3's and 4's (sure to be left) and substitute, therefor, the bright, shiny, New Brunswick sandals in their place. It gives all the advantages of individual cartons with none of their annoyances. (If this is not plain I will cheerfully furnish plans free.)

As a good workman requires good tools, so a fine stock of shoes requires fine fixtures and substantial, if not elegant, surroundings. But all this outlay of clerk hire, rent, etc., is of little use unless the people are made aware of the advantages offered.

Advertising, then, should not be classed with ordinary expense, which should always be kept at a minimum. For without it, in some form or another, business dies. The only query in the matter is, which is the best plan to follow, for all admit its necessity. Some claim that honesty and square dealing will succeed alone. Others contend that low prices will attract trade, and that printer's ink is unnecessary. The latter species, however, is nearly extinct. The retail shoe dealer, in fact, has a larger and more varied field to glean from than most other business, for every person who wears shoes is a possible customer, and he (the dealer) needs only to offer attractions to secure their trade. To offer those inducements through mediums which will attract the most people, therefore, is the problem for each merchant himself to solve. It must be determined from experiments, observations, and careful attention to the detail, for advertising has become an art, and must be studied as carefully as any other branch of management.

Fourthly and lastly, we come to the practical or business end of the management, viz.: selling. This is the most difficult subject to treat, and about which one can no more lay down rules than tell how to court a young lady. The customer must be treated

according to his or her moods, never twice alike.
The two most important plans of action are honesty and courtesy. Deal honestly with each and
every one, as three-fifths of the shoe trade either express or plainly imply their confidence in the judgment of the person serving them, or in the reputation of the house. When that confidence is ever impaired or destroyed, the trade is proportionately diminished or lost.

Politeness is as much a necessity nowadays as light
is for an evening trade. Make it a point to humor
each whim, or express a willingness to do so. It
pays. It is well to have but few "cast iron rules," that
is for the average business man who cannot afford to
assert his independence to the loss of his patrons.

Sell for "spot cash," if you can afford to do without the credit customer who brings with him a hundred-fold more influence than the "bargain-hunter."
The great mistake in most credit concerns is lack of
system in this department. Prompt, courteous collectors will offend fewer customers and lose a smaller
per cent than the slack pay-when-you-please plan.

Thus, the great problem can be worked to a successful solution by careful and systematic buying, by
systematic and attractive arrangement, by attractive
and plentiful advertising. and by plentiful and profitable selling ; and as your bank account waxes greater,
so will your circle of friends increase, and they will
all vote that the shoe business is a success.

How to Manage a Retail Shoe Store.

BY M. E. KREIDLER, WITH G. W. RHOAD, SOUTH BETH-
LEHEM, PA.

In my case the old saying, "Better late than
never," will hold good. As manager of the largest
retail establishment in our vicinity, my whole time and
energies are devoted to trying to reach the highest
standard attainable. Our business is all in departments. My lot—boots and shoes—am aware that
your excellent paper contains frequent communica-
tions unfavorable to dry good stores handling or retailing boots and shoes. Prejudice is what does it.
Time alone will remove it. With your permission I
will express my views through the columns of the
RECORDER on "How to Manage a Retail Shoe Store."

Location is one of the most important points. If
not fortunate enough to own the building in which to
do business, so as to be enabled to choose, it is policy
to select a locality where houses command a high
rental, for here you will invariably find business centers ; whereas cheap rents generally locate you where
you could ill afford to pay even a low rent. Do not
understand me to advocate high rents merely for the
name. Experience has taught that you might as

well be out of business when you have the wrong
location.

Exterior and interior of your store should receive
careful attention. Have everything about you look
neat and tasty, and as inviting as possible, thus showing your patrons that you appreciate their patronage.
The interior arrangements should receive special attention, in the way of mats, chairs, etc. When
starting in business we must consider that we are
public servants, and cater not entirely for one class
of trade but for all, the high and low, rich and poor.
With business tact both can be held and supplied.

We are placed in a store, a synopsis of the inside
of which may not be amiss. All hard wood finished
(ash), settees, chairs, stools, etc., should correspond.
Have two departments, ladies' and gents', in each of
which have ample room to again have misses', children's, boys' and youths' departments. We have an
eighteen foot ceiling which gives splendid room for
display in the way of shoe cartons, pictures, etc.,
which greatly adds to the general appearance, also
allows free ventilation. Shelves all should be made
movable. The following dimensions are well adapted
where no counters are used : Height of shelf from
floor, 7 feet 2 in. ; depth, 23 in. with a 13 in. ledge to
show goods ; first shelf, 12 to 14 in., to allow for boxes
to hold shoes not in cartons ; second and third
shelves 19 high, just what six average shoe cartons
will require in height. Figure over the depth and you
will find that six more can be placed in the back,
making twelve cartons in a small space ; no stock

room is necessary, as you have your entire capital before you. This gives you the best way imaginable to keep stock clean and never out of sizes. Points never to be overlooked. Same in gents' department : for instance, we have boot drawers on rollers holding 24 pairs, with partition, thus allowing two kinds standing up, no crushing. Men's and boys' heavy goods we have in similar drawers, holding forty-eight to sixty pairs, each drawer labeled or a holder attached with sample of contents. These fixtures must be used and seen to be appreciated. Convenience aids in many ways ; "A place for everything and everything in its place," is a true maxim.

We have two colors in cartons, one for ladies and the other for gents. All of these look uniform, and each one bears our name. The best advertisement you can get is a white label with size, kind and price plainly written thereon, telling at a glance what each contains.

Displaying goods is very important. Windows, show cases, etc., should have careful attention.

In buying goods, success greatly depends upon how and where you buy. Ample capital is what we all should have. At least, enough to discount all purchases, thus securing lowest prices. Solid substantial goods make more friends than shoddy ones, even though the latter can be sold at a less price. Buy the bulk of your goods from manufacturers. Have your own name with a brand placed on the sole of the shoe or in top facing, after you find a line to meet your wants in fit and wear. In this way you can have your own specialties, and derive the benefit of advertising instead of the manufacturer. For instance, take a ladies' kid shoe, say to retail at $1.75 ; brand " Reliable," push the shoe for all it is worth, that is, if convinced that you can stand back of it. Thus, throughout your entire stock bring the brands prominently before the public by judicious advertising in your home papers, stating in plain language all you claim. Be sure never to advertise that which you do not carry in stock, as is the case so often.

Shoe cuts, representing your different brands, are very convenient in getting up yearly catalogues in form of small books, giving a full description of all your special brands. Distribute these carefully, and you will reap the benefits in the way of increased sales. Every dollar invested in this way pays threefold. Mark goods in plain figures, and at just what you think you should or must have, making it a point never to deviate from a price once made, unless you want to close out a certain line. All such should have a separate place, making price such as to insure sale.

Estimating profits, or percentage at which goods ought to be sold, is, I think, the most trying question. Your sales and competition must to a great extent be your guide. Where gross profits on sales are the lowest, it will require that at least four times as much be sold yearly as the stock of goods kept, to make the business profitable. Suppose the gross profits to be 15 per cent, four times this will be 60 per cent of the stock, which, if $10,000, will show a net profit of

$6,000. If, however, there are any doubts of the ability to sell four times the amount of stock, and you think that not over three times the amount can be sold in a year, or $30,000, which would show a total profit, at the same ratio of only $4,500 net over and above expenses. This may be sufficient ; still, if the profit could be increased to 20 per cent on the goods sold, the result will be the same as in the first instance. The oftener the stock is in mercantile parlance, turned over, the cheaper the dealer can afford to sell his goods. One of the ways by which a business frequently becomes less profitable is through the accumulation of undesirable goods, which are seldom sold, on account of which yearly sales, though possibly not reduced in amount, are largely reduced in proportion to the stock of goods kept. The following table will show at a glance the relative advantages of large sales in proportion to the stock. It is made on the basis of a $10,000 stock, such as given to make the yearly profit of $6,000. It shows what percentage of profits is required.

	Sales.	Per cent.
If turned once a year,	$10,000	60
" " twice " "	20,000	30
" " three " "	30,000	20
" " four " "	40,000	15
" " five " "	50,000	12
" " six " "	60,000	10

Instances are frequent where retailers turn over their stock as often as twelve times in a year. There are others who do not turn their stock over more than once. The former prosper, the latter grow poorer.

Study the above table carefully, it will show you the secret of making money by selling at small profits.

Selling goods for cash is the simplest form in which business can be transacted, and wherever it is possible to do sufficient in this way, it will prove in the end most profitable. A cash business has two sides, and many fail of success because they only attend to one of them. It is quite as essential that the dealer buys for cash as that he sells for cash. If he does not, his chances of successfully competing with those who give credit are very limited. Should any retailer be so situated as not to be able to do a cash business, and must do a credit business, he will if he is prudent set a limit to the amount he will place out on credit. This limit should be proportioned to the amount of capital. A great deal may be done by a vigilant trader to save himself from loss by looking closely after the debtor after the credit is given. The debt should be due on some fixed day, so that the dealer may know when to ask for it.

Polite and competent clerks (which means consid_erable) or none, and salary has a great deal to do in securing such. If you are fortunate enough to have good trustworthy clerks, you have the most essential fixture in the store and may be considered as a large portion of your capital, as the result of each year's business is bound to show. The proprietor is, however, the best salesman, generally speaking. He should absent himself from business only in case of necessity. Personal overseeing will prove beneficial. He should keep himself thoroughly posted as to prices and styles, and continually note the wants of his trade. To gain knowledge of these subscribe for a real live shoe paper. The BOOT AND SHOE RE-CORDER is the best investment.

My views are thus given, and I trust that some of your numerous readers, by following some of the points given, may derive and realize the same amount of benefit that we did from the others. This is my sincere wish.

How to Manage a Retail Shoe Store.

BY " JOHN DOE OF DOEVILLE."

The writer has neither had a very long nor a very short experience as a retail dealer in boots and shoes, and does not claim to know enough about the business to place his name before the fraternity. But I have learned some things that I think may be of benefit to new beginners. They will cost nothing, and may be considered of a little value.

There are several points that should not be overlooked when contemplating organizing this branch of business :

1st. Do not attempt it unless you know how to handle a boot or shoe. If you don't know any better, then when you take up a boot the first thing you do is to commence pulling the crimping out. Or, if you don't know that the sun, heat from the stove and dust are just as injurious to boots and shoes as they are to dry goods, then keep out of the business.

2d. Buying. I don't buy of everything there is in the market, but select (according to the amount of stock I intend to keep) from two to six lines of ladies' goods, and buy misses' and children's of the same styles.

3d. How to handle goods when in single cartons.

Have separate departments for kid and goat goods.
Have the shelves twelve inches wide and ten inches
apart. Commence with kid button, the widest in
stock of all grades you handle, and place first on the
lower shelf the largest size, one above the other,
and so on down until you reach No. $2\frac{1}{2}$. Then fill
the next shelf above with next widest, and so on until all the kid button goods have found a place.

4th. Fill the departments for ladies' goat button,
ladies' kid and goat bals. and misses' goods in the
same manner.

5th. Have a department for each kind of goods
which are put up in single cartons, and arrange them
in the manner given. Then, when your customer
calls for a certain size and kind of shoe, you know
exactly where to find it, and can at once place before
him or her all the grades you have of the goods
called for.

6th. Much labor can be saved in handling children's shoes. Place one or more pairs of all kinds of
the heel shoes, sizes 1 and $1\frac{1}{2}$ in a common size carton, all kinds 2 and $2\frac{1}{2}$ in another, and so on until
all are provided with a place. Then place the cartons on the shelves one above another, and designate
the size by a conspicuous figure, and the style by a
shoe on the outside.

7th. Place children's fine heel shoes in the same
manner, with another lot of cartons for a heavier
grade of children's shoes.

8th. Distribute ladies' serge congress, that come
in large cartons, in the same manner.

9th. Keep rubber goods in drawers, and put in no more sizes in a drawer than you can keep separate· In this way you can select the size called for without overhauling the whole.

10th. Men's department. In handling boots introduce the boot case described in the RECORDER of July 15, 1885. I have tried it and have found it to be an excellent arrangement. For men's and boys' cartoned goods have your shelves fourteen inches wide and fourteen inches apart, and pursue the same course in placing goods as given for the ladies' department. Keep the various kinds of men's and boys' common goods separated as to sizes. By adopting these rules you can in a few minutes' time ascertain the sizes of all goods in stock.

Never add to your stock until you have made a memorandum of the sizes you need, and never buy of a party who will not give you the sizes asked for.

Have a neat tidy place with Soller's patent foot rests, one for ladies and the other for gents to try on goods. Use a good button machine for putting on buttons, and make it a part of the contract in selling that you will put on all buttons that come off, as long as the shoes need buttons.

Never get angry, even if a customer may tell you that he knows more about shoes than you do, and that he can buy cheaper at retail than you can at wholesale. Always seemingly keep good-natured. Trust just as little as possible ; better cry over your goods than after them.

I believe in printers' ink, that is, advertising. But

don't advertise more than you have got, and thus dis-
gust the first customer that comes into your store.
If you use the newspaper don't put in a long fine
type advertisement that nobody ever reads, and keep
it there for months, but insert a short, conspicuous
one and change it every week ; then people will look
each week to see what you have to sell.

Have a show case in the center of your store filled
with samples of goods. Don't put goods in the window to be burnt up in the sun, but place in the windows shoe cuts furnished in supplements by the Boot
and Shoe Recorder. They make a better show
than the shoes would, and the sun will not hurt them.

Keep your store neat and divested of cobwebs,
well-lighted by day and evening. Have a place for
everything and everything in its place. Represent
goods just as you think them to be, and be honest
with your patrons. Make them feel at home when
they visit your store. ' And last, though not least, sell
them all the goods you carry at live-and-let-live
prices, and the chances are that you will live long and
be happy.

How to Manage a Retail Shoe Store.

BY C. G. BRIGHT, AARONSBURG, PA.

I have read the letters on " How to Manage a Retail Shoe Store " from week to week ever since the prize competition has been opened. The letters in general are interesting and a few very beneficial to to the average country boot and shoe dealer. There is a great deal of sameness in the general expression of the letters already published. Why should they not be, there is but one proper basis upon which the management of a retail boot and shoe store can be placed in order to do a pleasant and successful business. Pleasant did I say? Why, my dear reader, if the business is not a pleasure to you, how do you expect to impart trust or confidence to your patrons. Always bear in mind that you are considered a man of distinction, under whose protection your customer places himself, therefore you must be courteous, polite, almost well-bred, being of elegant manners, civil, obliging, condescending. The book of human nature is an unbound volume, and has no final. These are the leaves (gathered from human nature) that you and I are called upon to arrange to suit our purpose. We can certainly arrange a part of these leaves and form a book sufficiently large to consume the time between business hours. Let us take up the great lesson of human nature, make it our daily study, and our crown will and must bear the inscription "Success belongs to this house." How much there is in the words "Thank you," "If you please," and the simple conjunctive words "Come again." Only two words so closely connected, containing such a vast meaning, and not one in the eighteen past essays contains this friendly invitation to " Come again." The writer, while visiting in the central part of Kansas in the summer of 1884, had the privilege of listening to the settlement of a difficulty that arose from a misunderstanding in a sale of goods between a clerk and his customer. The proprietor of the store was called to take charge of the case. How carefully he managed his side of the question. Cool and self-possessed, he brought his man to bay, and with a curse on his lips, the latter left the store with the words " Come again," ringing in his ears. What was the result of the separation? A return of the customer on the following day, satisfied that he was welcome after spurting forth the worst kind of abuse, such as you would expect from a Kansas ruffian. To the use of these two words, " Come again," I attributed the greater part of my success. While not all are approached in the same way upon entering the store, it is a fact that all will allow you, and the majority expect you to invite them back again. Did you ever take notice how common it is in a controversy for each to strive to have the last word? What do you give and expect in return from your customer when he is leaving your store; the last word. In extending the kind invitation to return, you carry your answer to him, which will be either a "Thank you," or "I will."

If your neighbor or a friend pays you a family call, upon leaving you invite him back again, why not do so when he calls at your place of business, whether he comes to make a purchase or not. This rule is applicable to all classes and conditions of customers.

The arrangement of your stock is a work which, if you once have the good-will and confidence of your customers is very easily done. The question in my mind is this, if you arrange your goods to suit your eyes, will it meet with the same approval of your customers. I always like to see a feeling between the merchant and his customer that creates a desire to be in each other's company. A pleasant and sociable man will always have company. Don't be afraid to ask the advice and opinion of a friend in the placing of your goods. When a customer drops in to see how you are getting along, not to buy, man or woman, allow him or her to take up a carton and place it for you, while you will stand off and see how it " strikes " you ; if passable be satisfied with the arrangement. That man or woman will go away, and by allowing them that little kindness, will advertise your business in a way that would otherwise cost you considerable. By giving each customer (voluntarily) a little work to do, your stock is arranged, and in nine cases out of every ten, all are satisfied. The classification of the goods will take place while the arrangement is made. Classification belongs to convenience, and that alone is for yourself at part of which your customer is not concerned. Goods placed in a position to suit your customers are always attractive. Convince your people by your conduct towards them that they are welcome, your business will be a pleasure to you and your patrons, and you are on the right way to build up a substantial trade. In this way your stock is arranged and the first and best advertisement made.

A few thoughts on quality, quantity and style of goods, taking the three collectively. We will now try and build up for ourselves a country trade. We first take into consideration the country our people are obliged to travel over. It is a mistaken idea that some dealers have that the heavier grade of shoes are calculated only for country wear. I have reference more particularly to the ladies' shoes, or to the class who are expected to wear the finest and highest priced goods. Taking the heavy shoe for the best wear, reminds me of a farmer in our locality going to the carriage maker to buy a pleasure carriage. After considering beauty and style, next come strength and durability. Invariably the farmer will ask for a heavy wheel. It is a fact substantiated by first-class carriage builders, that a light wheel made of the best material will give more and better service than a heavy wheel made of inferior material. The spokes and felloes of a light wheel to be serviceable are taken from trees of a few years growth, which by nature are tough, while the heavy wheel is taken from

trees of older growth and are naturally more brittle.
In leather (nearly all kinds) we find the same material difference, the best grades of goods are made of
light skins, and pliable, and will yield more readily
to any outside pressure, while the heavier grades are
made of heavy and coarse material, are hard and
brash, and, therefore, do not contain the strength and
wear of the lighter skins. Living among and trading
with country people I find that the finest and highest
priced goods bought from responsible manufacturers
give better satisfaction generally than the coarser and
cheaper grades. Buy several lines of good shoes
and you will have all that is necessary. These same
shoes, varying somewhat in style, you will carry in
narrow and wide bottom, narrow and wide toe, low
and high heel, heavy and light sole, all made from the
same material and bought from the same manufacturer. One principle object I have in view wherever
I talk shoes is, low heels and wide toes, in short common sense bottoms ; in this your customer secures
comfort and wear, and the dealer the assurance that
the corn and bunion trade will grow less, and the second order for a pair of shoes is guaranteed.

Shop-worn goods, or an accumulation of unsalable goods is due to a want of the proper knowledge
of the needs of your customers, and a want of practical knowledge of the material your goods are made
from. To prevent an accumulation of the above
kinds of goods, study the needs and wants of your
customers, read regularly every week the BOOT AND
SHOE RECORDER in which the inferior and superior

qualities of all classes of shoe leather are fully described ; by doing this you will be prepared to buy a stock of goods that will leave your shelves just as the change of seasons of the year will demand a change of footwear.

Supplementary Series.

ESSAYS PUBLISHED IN RESPONSE TO A SECOND OFFER
OF PRIZES ON SAME SUBJECT.

DEALERS WHO DESIRED TO COMPETE BUT WHO WERE
NOT IN TIME FOR FIRST SERIES.

ADDITIONAL POINTS OF VALUE TO ALL DEALERS ON
THE DETAILS OF SHOE STORE MANAGEMENT.
IN THE ORDER AS PUBLISHED.

How to Manage a Retail Shoe Store.

BY "OLD CALFSKIN," (G. N. FINK,) SALEM, O.

By your request to all subscribers of the RECORDER, to write on "How to Manage a Retail Shoe Store," I will give my opinion, and if you think well of the article publish it in this week's issue, if not, throw it in your waste basket and all is well.

In managing a boot and shoe store the first thing is, do we expect to make money, or do we expect to only make a living? Why is it that so many good business men who invest in the selling of boots and shoes fail? Is it because they are not qualified for the business, or is it because they are not in possession of sufficient means to carry out what they undertake. Very few men who fail, fail to make money; neither do they fail because they are not qualified for the business. Of course there are exceptions to this, but, as a rule, they fail for want of capital to carry out what they undertake. In my estimation no man should invest in the selling of boots and shoes unless he has a capital of $5,000. Better have $10,000. With a less capital than that better go into a small business in some other line. To sell boots and shoes and make money, that amount is sufficient to justify

a man so that he may have accumulated a good
round pile for old age. If he has this amount then
"go in, Muggins."

What comes next? Five years experience as a
boot and shoe clerk, or a clerk at other business for
that length of time, better boots and shoes.

Why? To study human nature; this is a great essential, and one of the greatest parts of business.
Now, if he has the money, and the experience in clerk-
ing, then he may go ahead, and if he will follow the
following rules he will be sure of success, and don't
you forget it.

Location is very essential. The appearance of the
room does not make so much difference as some people may suppose. Better have a good location and a
poor room, than a good room and a poor location.
Then buy goods for cash only to the amount of your
cap'tal. Buy good, substantial, all - leather goods.
Never put any shoddy in stock; better lose the sale
on a customer than to lose the influence and good-
will. Buy mostly in medium-priced goods, well made
and of a good reliable factory. Carry some good
high-priced goods to suit the finer class of trade.
But look out, only just sufficient to meet the demand,
for in fine goods comes the loss, if any, in old stock,
and of course there will be some. As seasons change
and goods go out of style, you will have some left
over, and you cannot help it. These goods put on
your counter and sell at cost. For instance, a $3, $4
or $5 counter, as it may be, and make an effort to
close them out as fast as possible. Better lose on

the first year after they are out of style than to hold
on to old goods, for they depreciate fast. Never refuse an offer on old stock, if it is any way reasonable.
Show up the old goods. New goods sell themselves,
and it takes a salesman to sell old stock.

Now, so far as managing stock is concerned, there
has been enough said. My motto is, arrange your
stock to suit yourself, for there are not two stores in
fifty who arrange the same   But put your goods in
such a manner so you know where everything is, and
any man who has any business to invest in a shoe
store has certainly enough energy to find what he has
to sell, and if he has not then he had better stay out
of the business. It is not so much how the stock is
arranged as the kind of stock to arrange ; but keep
your stock clean. Take account of stock twice a
year, and I dare say any clerk of much intelligence
will know where it is ; if he does not he should.

Now comes the credit business, the curse to all retail boot and shoe men who engage in it. Sell strictly
for cash. Make it a rule, and for God's sake stick to
it. Get the cash for every dollar's worth of goods
that goes out, or keep your goods. Throw out inducements to cash buyers.

How ? Take an article, something good, sell it at
cost.

Why ? To get cash trade to advertise you ; don't
expect to make profits on all goods alike, for if you
do you are going to get left in this day of doing a shoe
business. For instance, make it a rule on all goods
to add 5 per cent to cover freight and small expense,

then add 30 per cent straight through the stock, with the exceptions of a few leaders which you will sell at cost 5 per cent added.

Now advertise. How? Any way to reach the most people. Don't be afraid to say what you think, but back up what you say. Don't let any one in the trade try to injure you through stories without returning them with interest. Don't bother any competitor. Stay in your own store. Run your own business, and let people know you mean business. Use all customers well, but at the same time do not overdo it. Make all clerks hold their tempers, proprietor not excepted. Never get out of patience no matter how badly your customers use you, but politely say, "Come again, we will use you as well as we can." Take an awful site of abuse and give in return pleasant words, for kind words never die.

The man to run a shoe store successfully must have the patience of Job. Don't sit around with a long face because trade is dull. Look pleasant, talk pleasant, and not only to the bon ton, but to all classes of people. Make yourself the friend of every person you can.

Mark your goods with tags, it is better, does not soil the bottoms. Mark in plain figures the selling price. Always ask the price marked to every one.

Look out for staples, such as carpet slippers, lasting slippers and a few of the little lines of goods which are known by customers. Sell this class of goods low, and make your leaders on this line of goods mostly. Customers know these lines of goods, but know little about the other kinds.

Run a one-price store and you will soon have the confidence of the trade; to lose the confidence of the people is the worst thing to do, and that you will surely do unless you sell at one price. But be careful. People cannot tell the exact value of 25 to 30 cents on a pair of good shoes, while you can. Should your shoes now and then be a little higher than your neighbor may be selling, you have a chance to display in such a case your salesmanship by talking quality, but on goods which the trade know the value well, such as slippers of cloth or carpet, mark down so low that you know you cannot be beaten. These rules invariably hold good.

Don't warrant any goods only as they are. This warranting business is the worst thing you can do. Only warrant them to be as represented, and represent the goods just as they are. Tell the trade you will give them your experience, and that is all you can do. Make the factories stand by just what they represent the goods to be, and nothing else.

Never order goods unless you want them, and when you order take them, unless they are not what you ordered, and then don't ship back until notifying the house. Use the factory or house well that you buy of, for you owe to them, to a great extent, your success. Always be kind to traveling men. Look through their goods, but don't be persuaded unless it is a matter of business. Don't let them overload you with goods, for that they will surely do unless very careful. Many a man has gone down by over-stock. Don't trust your business to clerks but attend to your own business as much as possible, so that other people may have time to attend to their business. Be punctual, make your word as good as your bond, and by the powers you are bound to succeed.

Have energy, lots of it, and, if you have none, take a good tonic, for it takes push, push, push all the time to sell goods for cash, and sell enough to make money. By giving credit it is easy to sell goods, but everlasting death, everlasting death, everlasting death.

P. S. I have sold shoes for ten years, and the above principles have been my motto. I have made money and expect to make more.

How to Manage a Retail Shoe Store.

BY J. MARKS, CHARLESTOWN, S. C.

To advise others how to attend and how to run a
shoe store, is easy enough on paper, but it does not
turn out so when you start to open a shoe store yourself with your own capital. In my opinion there is
only one way, that must be the right way. I will not
take the responsibility of advising others what to do
but will give a few points that may be perhaps interesting to some as to how things are carried on in my
establishment, which is perhaps no comparison in
size and amount of stock or of sales to what others
do and have.

Some persons have very good ideas, but not enough
capital ; others have the contrary. I have read your
valuable journal which reaches me on Saturday, and I
lose no time in reading each and every article it contains, both reading matter as well as advertisements.

I have learned considerable since I became one
of your subscribers, and don't see how anyone in the
shoe trade can do without it. I have read nearly
every article you have placed before your readers on
the subject of to " How to Manage a Shoe Store."

I differ with a great many, perhaps I am wrong ; if
I am wrong I will confess I am young and willing to

be reprimanded. Some one advertised that he sold shoes on credit; that was his style of business, but I will come in conflict with him on this very point. I would not advise anyone to do any kind of retail trade on a credit system. My mode of doing business is the main principal that I work on which is "T. O. T." It means cash every time. I do business in a store 80 feet deep by 18 feet wide, shelves on both sides and counter shelves wide enough to lay cartons on while showing stock. The floor is carpeted from front to rear, and in the center I have 48 chairs suitable for a shoe store with suitable mats and stools arranged. I have two large windows one on each side, inside of which I have nickel plated fixtures with five circular shelves on each side, upon which I display my shoes, and the same revolve by electricity, thereby displaying all the shoes on the stands to a great advantage. My stock on the shelves is in rotation from the smallest size up, so when a customer comes in there is no delay in finding the size. Each pair is mate marked and the price on each pair. My motto is, "One price to All." In showing your goods always start with the low priced and advance as your customer will express his or her wishes in the mean time to you.

When a child comes for a pair of shoes accompanied with, or without a parent, you want to take the shoe off the first thing and try a pair on, then you will succeed every time in selling. You don't want to let customers button their shoes themselves, especially the shoes they are trying on. Nine times out of ten you will find the buttonholes have been strained where they are too tight. In this section we cannot take the shoe off a lady as she sits down like they do North, they would not a'low it. When you see customers entering the store you must walk right up to them and not stand back for them to come to you.

In showing shoes don't show any style of which you have not the size, but show several styles to select from, then you will find that sales are always effected with ease. Have your clerks to be polite. See that they wear good shoes and always blackened, and have them blackened before coming to the store.

Attend to your own business only, and leave others alone. Don't be jealous of your neighbors. Don't try to do all, for it is impossible. Take it easy. Keep your store clean. Don't try to be economical, it has a tendency to keep trade away. Use plenty of lights, burn gas if you can get it. Adverti e your business for all it is worth, for trying to do business without advertising is like the fellow who was winking at a girl in the dark, he knew what he was doing, but no one else did. The poor when they die take along just as much as the rich. Keep your store in apple-pie order. Look at the samples of every commercial traveler who may offer to show them to you. You can only improve by it. You don't need to buy from each one. Don't buy too much at any one time. Consider how much your sales are and how much you can discount. You can always get shoes ; the country is large. Stay in one place until you become known. Sell at a reasonable profit. Don't do like some who want $2 for a shoe that cost $1.25, they want to get rich suddenly and eventually fail. I keep the Peninsular Button Machine. I fasten on buttons on all shoes no matter who sells them, drive nails in the heels, take off lifts, stretch shoes and don't charge for it. It don't cost anything, and in the end it pays you. When a pair of shoes is returned to me for obvious reasons and the party don't want any other kind, I invariably return the money without any comments or delay. It does your business more good than you would gain otherwise. It is not all profit, and such cases do not happen more than once a week. By refusing to refund the money that individual customer is not what you lose, but his friends collectively will do more injury than the pair of shoes is worth. I will not deprive you of too much space and trust you will place this before your readers. It is not for any prize that I desire to teach others who may be more capable of instructing the trade, but if they can beat me running a shoe store they would have to get up earlier than I do in the morning, and I am up all night. If all shoe dealers in the retail trade will only do as your writer, they will never have cause to complain, while I am rusticating among the earthquakes by the sea.

How to Manage a Retail Shoe Store.

BY W. B. RICE, CARLISLE, PA.

I have read with vast amount of pleasure and profit the different essays on this subject, and I desire to thank the RECORDER for the forethought and the enterprise it displayed in opening this mutual interchange of thought, which can't help but be beneficial to all retail dealers in the country.

I desire to add my contribution and to give you some qualifications, which I think absolutely essential to every dealer, who wishes to make a success of his business.

First and foremost he must have capital, capital sufficient to buy his first stock for cash. It seems to me that it is useless for a man without means to enter in any business, let alone the shoe business. He ought to certainly have some capital to back his business with, or he will surely fail. This I think is self-evident and needs no further comment.

In the next place a man must have had some experience in the business, or alas for the shoes that he buys. The best teacher is experience, and if you can't tell the difference between a calfskin and a buff leather shoe, our advice is stay out of the business. We have seen men drifting from one business to

another, notably from a dry good store to a shoe store,
We have seen these stand up and praise shoes made
out of paper, we might say. Drummers came to them.
talked up their shoes, these men bought them for first-
class goods, and when they sold them to their customers they were honest in their assertions, yet at the
same time they deceived their customers because they
did't know any better. They had no experience.

Again, when you receive your goods you must have
some place to put them, so as to show them off to
the best advantage. And where do you want to put
them? Why, in a nice, convenient, moderately large,
centrally located room, where lots of people pass
daily, and where every body knows there is a shoe
store. Keep the outside and inside of it attractive
and inviting. Have a large show window and a
couple of glass cases on the outside filled with samples of your goods. In the inside let the shoes be
arranged in boxes on the shelves, and place a label
on them marking the prices. Keep your shoes in
good order. Have your room well lighted, warm and
convenient, and on every side give it the appearance
of attractiveness and cheerfulness. Have separate
apartments for ladies and gentlemen, and have comfortable chairs in them, and if possible have the whole
room carpeted. If not the whole room, by all means
have the apartments where the shoes are tri d on
carpeted.

As to the stock of shoes to carry, you want to keep
as few lines of shoes as possible. For your rich customers the best line of shoes, for laborers and farmers

not such a stylish line, but a strong and substantial one. If there is a shoe factory in your town or city, make a specialty of their shoes, and right in your store-room have a workman to make shoes to order. Some people are very hard to fit ; others have a natural liking for home-made work, and for these it pays to keep a good shoemaker in your store.

Again you want to let people know that you sell goods kept by you alone. You want to make and keep a reputation for selling a certain line of goods. Advertise them well both in circulars and newspapers. Don't, I beseech you, don't be afraid of printer's ink. Keep constantly in the papers an advertisement, and have a regular place for it. Be original, write your own advertisements, and write them so they'll attract attention. Stick to what you advertise, and let yonr reputation be such that when people read your ads they will know you mean what you say, and that you never go back on your word.

As I said in the beginning buy your goods for cash, and then when you come to sell always sell for cash. Don't trust any one, not even till Saturday night, for Saturday night will never come to some people. Tell people you buy for cash and you sell for cash, and make them stick to the rule : "Pay as you go, then you won't owe."

There is a great deal in arranging goods, but it depends somewhat on the stock you carry, the store you are in, and the trade you have. Don't be afraid to show goods. Purchasers oftentimes come in and they don't know what they want. It is your duty to tell them what they ought to have. Use a little strategy in your dealing. If a lady asks for a No. 2 and you know she wears a No. 4, give her No. 4. It is very likely she'll never know any better, and her feet will be comfortable and easy.

Of course traveling men will visit you often and they are always glad to see you. They'll want to sell you everything they have. Treat them kindly, look over their goods and chat with them. If they have anything you want or need, buy it, but don't buy everything because a drummer wants you to.

Strive to rise above your competitors and to keep above them. Don't sit still and frown and whine about hard times, but "be up and doing." Be energetic, enterprising and reliable. Put a price on your goods and stick to it. Mark them one price to the gentlemen of leisure and the workingman, to the merchant and the farmer, to the rich and the poor, and in this way establish your reputation for fair, honest business-like dealing. Be polite to all, speak to your customers on the street and give them friendly recognition everywhere, whether dressed in the rich garment of the millionaire or the noble garb of the day laborer. Don't be afraid of laying too much stress on politeness. Make your clerks practice it. How often you hear people say : " Yes, I know Jones keeps a good store, but I don't like that clerk of his. The last time I was there it seemed to be too mnch trouble and labor for him to show goods. If I knew Jones was in himself, I would go there, but I believe I'll go over to Smith's, where the proprietor and his clerks also always make you feel at home."

Welcome your customers with a kindly greeting, talk to ·them and always invite them back again. Make them feel you have confidence in your store and in yourself, and that you intend to make a success of your business. You say these things are trifles and they come naturally to a man in business. You say anyone who has a method or policy in his business knows and does these things. But we say the very triteness of them makes them too often over-looked. Don't regard them as trifles, for it is the attention to the little details and circumstances that makes success possible.

Keep good clerks, regard the quality rather than the quantity of them, and pay them good wages. If they are attentive to business, well disciplined and sharp dealers they earn every cent they get. And when you have spare time, don't run out and let the clerks run the place, but stay in and employ it all in fixing up yonr room, your window and your stock. Perhaps you have some old stock left over; keep it in good order, for some day some one who is just looking for that kind of goods will come in and buy them. Don't forget to sell them to him at cost. He may be one of your competitor's customers, but after that he is one no more.

Don't allow loafers in your store. Let the other fellows have them all. You can't afford to have them, for you have a reputation to maintain, therefore frown on all loafers.

And now in conclusion if to all these qualifications there is behind the counter a man of character and reputation for honor and intelligence, the winds and the storms of the opposition houses may beat upon his house, but it will stand. For it is built on a firm foundation and cannot fall.

How to Manage a Retail Shoe Store.

BY A HOOSIER, EVANSVILLE, IND.

Sins thair seams tu be sich a grate desire fur infur-mashun on the subjeckt of keepin a shoe stoar, I hav conkluded tu rite out a fu plane sejestins ov a pratiklel nater that may be adopted by enny one what haz the inclinashun and the munney.

Speakin ov munney reminds me that one ov the moast important artikcels in or about a shoe stoar iz munney; in fackt it iz imposibell tu hav a well rege-lated, fust-class stoar without it; and while al faleurez air not altogether doo tu a totel lack ov munney, yit fareminded peepel will bare me out in the assurshun that its gudishus use wood stave off a faleure fur a rite smart while.

The fackt that munney iz so mitey a fackter in the managment ov a shoe stoar shal be my excuce fur a fu words az tu how tu git anuff tu start on.

Borrerin haz always bin a very poplar method tu raze reddy cash, and I would sejest that ef you doant hapen to· hav $6000 or $7000 about you the best thing you kin doo iz tu borrer that mutch from sum relativ; your wife fur instunce.

The advantages ov borrerin ov your wife air tofould, fust, she woant charg enny intrust, and seckond, in case ov faleure the loss will be in the family.

Selecshun ov a stor iz next in order, after whitch I wood seject that a sivil inginear be imploid to run the seckshun lines and lokate the different departments; plases whare seats, rugs, rapin counter, stoav, water cooler, etc., air to be.

Doan't be to pertickler about fixin or git em tu fine, you mite in this way make the impreshun tha you air ritch and thairfoar crooel and proud, whitch mite make timid but dezervin people afeered tu ask trust, and in that way drive your trustin custemers away.

In the perchas of goods, buy ov az menny diferent houses az you can, your bils will be smaler and your variety grater, and you won't be bothered with so menny pares of a kind; but never under any sirkum-stanses shood you look at drumerz sampils til he iz compleatly humbilled by bein made to call at least six times while in your town; and then no matter how bad you want his goods, doan't give him your order tu wunst, but make him rare and charge around and claw the are awhile fust; that will make him think you air a bisiness man and he a grate sailsman.

Presumin that time anuff haz elapst sins I rit the last paragraff fur the goods to git in and be arainged and the bils tu be du, it becums my douty to give sum instrukshun az tu how tu pay bils. When a bil reeds terms nett cash in sixty days, that meens that you shal wate til you have had the goods in your stoar sixty days, and then you shal deduckt 5 per cent. and send on the balens. If the manufackterer doan't like it he kan say so.

Az fur clurcks giv em tu no fust, last and al the time that you air boss, make em no thare plase, drill em a hour eatch day in the maner ov reseavin and dismisin custemers, and passin remarks about wether.

Make it a pint and see tu it that no custemer be aloud to leve your stoar without having his or her attenshun called to the fackht that the wether iz hot or coald, or wet or dry, az the case may be, a omishun ov this may cost you sum ov the best trade in your town. When straingers air in your stoar, be shure tu speek tu your clurcks in sich a way az tu remoov enny dout az to ho iz boss ; otherwize ef one of your clurcks hapens to be better lookin than you air, or wairs better close than you do, you mite be mistuck fur a clurck, and the afoarsed clurck mite git the credit ov being proprietor, whitch wood be very harrowin to the feelins————of the clurck.

In watin on custemers give em to understand that your goods air supeerier tu al others and your prises lower. Speek ov competiters with a contemptshus snear, and intemate that az fur onesty, you air abuv suspishun, but al others in the shoe bizness air bace deceevers tetotally and bodashusly unworthy ov confidens.

If when you sho a lady a shoe, she shood be so audashus az tu say she doan't like it, and intemate a desire tu see sum other stile, doan't indulg hur in enny sich whims ; proseed tu wunst and argy hur into takin the shoe you fust tuck down ; tel hur that Mrs. Keernel So-and-So got a pare ov em jist now, and that Mrs. Gudge Somebody wares that sort al the time.

Another word and I am dun. Sum peepel sez that shoe dealers tel az menny lies about thare sails az cuntry editers tel about their sirculashun ; whether this be troo or fals iz not fur me tu say. I simply refur the matter tu a long sufferin publick. Howsumever, I wood say, that mutch az I despize lies, ef shoe dealers must lie about thare treemendus sails, tha shood compencate thare vicktims by saying that while the sails air grate, the profits are powerful smal.

How to Manage a Retail Shoe Store.

BY "CALIFORNIAN," (E. F. ROCKFELLOW,)

SAN DIEGO, CAL.

After reading two of your prize articles on "How to Manage a Retail Shoe Store," the writer will endeavor to give you his views on the subject. First, get the best location you can for the business, the matter of few dollars saved in rent, and being out of the main business part of the town does not pay. Get as near your competitors as possible, and make your store both inside and out as attractive as possible. Change your display in window or windows at least once a week, and never put the same pair of shoes back into the window. Neat shelving, not too high, is to be desired, just high enough to reach any carton in the shelves. Heavy moulding over shelving is not good, as it wastes too much valuable space to keep reserve stock on, and only makes the clerks climb higher to replenish regular stock. Drawers are a nuisance no matter how large or how small. Have two shelves below your ledge or projection twelve inches apart and about six inches from floor, to keep the reserve stock. On the two lower shelves and above the top shelf you have plenty of room for the reserve of goods. This all alludes to stock kept in cartons, and makes allowance for four shelf spaces

(165)

above the ledge nine to ten inches apart, with room
enough to hold three cartons of ladies' goods or two
of gent's. Keep only one pair of a size on your
regular stock shelving, and as they are sold replenish
from your reserve stock. Deep shelving is to be
avoided, as in stocking up you may think sometimes
that you have plenty of sizes back behind in reserve
when some of your clerks have placed them all out in
front. Always have every shoe you have in stock in
full view at all times. Put every boot and shoe you can
in cartons. The light stock boxes holding one dozen
pairs ladies' shoes are not all good, as all your goods
in them get more or less shopworn by continued handling. The same holds good for children's and infants'
lines. Save your empty cartons, especially in men's
goods, and put your calf boots in them ; they all come
in handy. Oftentimes you have a shipment of goods
come in where the cartons are all smashed up. In
such cases take the goods out, get good cartons and
put them in, and you will always have your stock neat.

Have nice gummed labels for all your cartons, with
a cut of the shoe or boot it contains. In ladies' wear
everything is button, and all you need is three lots of
labels with a cut of a high heel, low heel and spring
heel shoe. For men's you have congress, balmoral,
button, buckle, one or two styles for low shoes, opera
and calf leg boot, and one style for slippers. Ladies'
low shoes and slippers you can have as many styles
as you want. On your label you want to leave space
to print or write plainly the quality, as French kid,
calf, etc., size, width and price, which should always

be in plain figures. With such labels on your boxes you can find anything you want if the goods are properly placed, and once used you will never do without. For $25 to $30 enough labels can be furnished with cuts to last a year or more, and at same time will be worth the amount expended as an advertisement.

Have a place for all your goods. In your ladies' department keep all your ladies' French kids in one tier of shelves; next, your straight goat, Dongola, Tampico and Curacoa kids, pebble goat, calf, etc. Have all your low shoes and slippers together, arranged according to price. Then comes your misses', child's and infants' wear, which continually need care and attention to keep in sizes and styles; and here allow me to give my way of selling child's and misses'. Take, for instance, a ladies' pebble button that retails for $3; misses' shoe in the same quality would be worth $2.50; child's, 8 to 10½, $1.75 to $2; 5 to 7½, $1.50 to $1.60. Take the sizes like this: 5, 5½ and 6, $1,50; 6½, 7, 7½, $1.65; 8, 8½, 9, $1.75; 10, 10½, $2; 11, 11½, 12, $2.25; 12½, 13, 13½, $2.50; 1, 1½, 2, $2.75; ladies', $3, and all other misses' and child's shoes in same proportion; for when a child wears a 7½ shoe the next pair probably in three months or less must be No. 8, and if you tell them the price is $1.75, or 25 cents more than last pair, they complain. With my way the advance on the class of shoes mostly worn by children from 5 child's size to ladies size is never more than 25 cents, and have never had a complaint from this manner of marking misses' and children's goods for

past three years. Before this time I had frequent
complaints, and very often sold smallest sizes in a line
of goods for 25 cents less than they were worth, which
is that much loss, where by this way of marking three
half sizes at a price you get just what you want for
your shoes, and a child that wears a No. 11 shoe
should not pay as much for same as one that wears a
No. 2.

In men's department have one or two tiers of
shelves for congress, same for balmorals and button;
then comes boots. Keep all your calf boots in cartons, and have your space for them in shelving, with
your reserve above for two top shelves and below
for two bottom shelves. You will find you can carry
a good stock in a small room, using all the waste
space between top of shelving and the ceiling, and
always have your shelves filled. Men's heavy kip
boots I would keep in cartons also, as well as brogns
and plow shoes if could get a good carton made for
same, and keep reserve stock in back room or cellar,
in original cases. Here again comes work; you
must mark on outside of case the number of pairs in
it, also sizes, and have clerks be very particular to
note every pair they take out, or your label on case
will show several pairs of sizes on hand that are miss-
ing when you look for them.

Always buy from man facturers, and manufacturers
who manufacture for retail trade only, when you possibly can wait for them to make up your order, even
if you can buy the same shoe from a jobber at same
price. The jobber knows what you pay the manu-

facturer for the goods, and in buying in large lots he
can save a little on the shoe from the price you pay
for same ; but, as a rule, he is not satisfied with so
small a profit, and will have the shoe made with a
split innersole and counter, if not one out of these
pressed leather shavings, or if a hand-sewed shoe,
look and you will see the stitches are larger, especially
under the instep. If you will sell two pairs of shoes
to two of your customers, both same price shoe, one
from manufacturer, the other from a jobber, you will
see that the shoe from the jobber does not come up
to the other in wearing qualities at all. Buy the best
goods you can, and buy from one house as much as
possible. Stay with them as long as you can buy
from them as good goods and as cheap as you can
buy elsewhere. Don't buy three or four dozen pairs
from this one, and so on around from every traveler
that comes along. They are anxious to show goods
and to sell them. Look at all the samples you can,
and when you look at a line of goods compare them
in your mind with goods you have been buying elsewhere. If no better quality and no cheaper, it is very
easy to say, there is no need of buying as you can do
just as well from your old house. While staying with
your old house if you can sell goods enough for them,
you can have the exclusive sale of their goods, which
is a big thing for you, and you will have goods your
competitors cannot get, and will get better prices for
the same than you could get if all had the same goods.

In buying a shoe look at it. Suppose the price is
$4.25 and you know you can only get $5 for it, see if

you can't find a shoe at $4 that will sell just as quick
at $5. Always know you can sell the shoe at a profit
before you buy it. In figuring profits suppose you
want your sales to net you say 15 to 20 per cent.
profit; in this case many men I think make a mistake
and mark their whole stock to sell at 15 or 20 per
cent. advance straight through. You may have
bought some line of goods, or may have to carry some
lines where competition is so close they would not
pay 10 per cent, and you would not make your sales
bring the profits they should. Mark every shoe at a
price it will sell for, no matter if it is only 10 per cent;
don't keep holding it trying to get 15 or 20 per cent·
You will have other lines that will bring 25 and even 50
per cent.; mark them up to those prices. You are in
business to make money not for your health, and you
want to sell as cheap as you can and make a profit; but
if you have bought a bargain don't give it away unless it
was bought for a leader.

Have your name stamped on all goods you have
made, on the lining inside, that is if it is a shoe that
will give service, and your customer will come back for
the same shoe. Always advise your customers to buy
good goods, as you will have just as much complaint
from a poor wearing shoe at $2 as if it cost $7 or $8.
Carry just as little trash as possible (I call shoddy
goods trash).

Advertise; it pays if only to keep your name before
the public. Locals are good. Different localities
need different kinds of advertisements. Look into
your advertisements and you will soon see what kind
par he best, and keep it up.

Don't try to carry too large a stock ; try and make your sales larger each month without increasing your expenses, and without carrying too heavy a stock. Have good salesmen and pay good salaries. ˙ You can't get as good a man for $40 as you can for $60 or $75. Your cheap man will not look out for your interests like a man that gets a good salary, and oftentimes you get a man that will work for a starvation salary but will be dishonest every chance he gets.

Get good men, pay good salaries and treat your employes as your equals (which they are), and you will do well, and they will do well by you. If you drive them and complain about every sale they make, etc., etc., you will find that every minute you are out of the store they will shirk their work and do just as little as they possibly can. If you could read their thoughts it would be something like this :-"I am glad the old skinflint is gone. He stands over me and drives me all the time ; complains because I did not sell the last customer a pair of $2 or $3 shoes and charge him $5 for them. One thing is certain, I don't do anything I can help for him, and will quit as soon as I can find another place." Oftentimes it is worse than this. Be honest yourself in all your dealings, and you will set a good example for your employes. Oftentimes the employer leads the employes to be dishonest by learning them to cheat every customer they can, and after the salesman gets the habit thoroughly instilled he will say to himself : "Well, the old man wants me to misrepresent and cheat every-one, and he will cheat me, too. My only way to

keep even with him is to pocket every sale I can, because he swindles everyone he can, and will charge
me up with more of my salary that I have drawn."

Don't misrepresent anything. If your customer
calls for a No. 3 shoe of certain style which you happen to be short of, don't take a 3½ and try to
scratch off the ½, but say you only have 2½ or 3½
and try and sell it. Even if you miss a sale you are
better off in the end, for if you make a sale by re-mark-
ing the shoe your customer will be very likely to find
it out, or if she should not, next time she buys a pair
of shoes she may go to your competitor and call for
the No. she wears. He will look at the old shoe and
will be able to tell her that the shoe has been re-
marked or changed. The customer will say to herself, "Well, if he will do that he will do worse, and I will
not patronize him again." Be candid, and if you miss
the sale in first instance, the customer can say : "He
is a very pleasant man and seems to be honest, and I
will go back to him the next time I have a purchase
to make."

The former essays in this series that I have read, I
think have done me good, and I trust that what I have
said above will be of benefit to some of the readers of
same.

How to Manage a Retail Shoe Store.

BY U. U. KAYPEE, (W. K. PATRICK) URBANA, OHIO.

"A little house well filled.
A little farm well tilled.
A little wife well drilled."

In writing upon the subject of "How to Manage a Retail Shoe Store," I have, I assure you, no desire to be either thorough or profound. While discussing very much at random, the essentiality of what we call any principle purpose, it shall be my aim to cite for your consideration some few of those which suit my taste, or which upon my own fancy have left the most definite impression. Now, doubtless a large number of your readers, while disagreeing with me in many particulars, will agree with me upon, at least, one essential point, that next to the perplexing question "How to manage a wife," comes that equally engrossing one "How to manage one's business;" while women all differ as to which requires the most business tact.

I once heard a man say to another, "you ought to succeed, for you watch the little things." And that is just the point, no business can be successfully carried on without care in watching things both large and small closely. For great things, great successes or great failures have their origin in small beginnings; ergo closely scrutinize the small matters of every day

(173)

business life. It's the little leaks that eventually sink the largest ships.

In my travels I find that in some of the shoe stores, all counters, (save a wrapping counter, which might contain the till) are being eliminated. A good wide way shelf, permitting your customers to have access to your wares, affords a better opportunity for effecting sales. Shoes not being sold by the yard, I think counters are unnecessary.

There is one thing, I think, in which many of our shoe dealers are sadly remiss,, and that is not furnishing proper screens for ladies when trying on shoes. Now it is almost impossible as you know, for a lady to dress her feet without more or less elevating her clothing,, hence many a sale is lost by her taking one or two pairs home to try on, when if she could be induced to sit down, you could have the opportunity to keep "pulling down" till a fit is secured. And right here let me note a matter of the very highest importance, and that is, get your customer seated and the shoe off before commencing to show your shoes.

Three-fourths of the sales you lose would be made if this was more general'y observed. And if you find you are about to lose the sale after all, before the old shoe is buttoned up turn your customer over to another salesman, for a poor carpenter can clinch a nail driven already by a good one. As a last resort solicit the privilege of ordering a single pair from your manufacturer.

As regards window displays avoid having a too long run of the same thing. The public eye is a sensitive organ, and is quick to notice a change and remark the same, and soon wearies of monotony. Therefore, they shou'd be changed at least twice a week and fresh novelties added. A window which contains gent's shoes one week might show ladies' the next, and vice versa.

Keep your best shoes at the front of your store, for first impressions are favorable or unfavorable and lasting, but "size up" your customer before showing a high or low priced article.

Have each kind and size of shoe in one box or row, commencing with the smallest size at top, numerical pyramid, as it were. I have my stock thus kept, and I am able to go with my eyes shut and place my hand on anything wanted. Another advantage thus ga'ned is that you can effect a sale by showing but two or three pairs. Nothing confuses a person so much as the showing of too many goods. Many a sale is so lost. This was the trouble Mark Twain had in buying his jack knife.

Never misrepresent a boot or shoe. Tell the truth about them even if you lose a sale thereby. It will be money to you afterwards, for that gentleman or lady knows he or she can get what they are getting, and will have no fear of sending their children alone for their footwear. They will know that no undue advantage will be taken of them.

Find out what your customer wants before commenting on the boots or shoes shown, and if you are satisfied you can, try and work off your "store keeper's," old shop-worn goods, but do not attempt this with your regular customers; they know what they want and are always willing to pay the price of a good article. Still sell at a profit if possible at all times, but let your old goods go, even if at one-fourth their cost.

When a drummer enters your place of business remember he is a man, or is supposed to be, and treat him as such, even if you don't want to buy, and even then look at his wares, for it costs you nothing and you may be able to learn something. If you see anything that is favorable, take a memorandum, which the agent no doubt will be glad to leave with you. You may want just these goods a little later, and like the Texan with his pistol, you may want them bad.

Permit no loafing or smoking about your store. I have seen ladies pass by a shoe store, when such things were permitted, rather than be subjected to the annoyance. Politely request them to retire to the office or sidewalk with their cigars and cigarettes.

One of the most certain stepping stones to ultimate success is persistent and judicious advertising. I have tried all ways, and finding nothing to equal a good size space in our city and country papers. Ten dollars thus expended will equal fifty dollars in finer and chromo advertisments. As much expended for printer's ink as for clerk hire would be money well invested.

If possible consummate a local organization with your neighbors, and thus protect yourself against the "Beats" who seem to invest every community.

Make it a rule to invariably give a receipt for every dollar received on account. Before I adopted this rule I was swind.ed out of no little amount by reputable(?) parties claiming to have paid. If you make it a rule to give receipt, this game is effectually stopped.

Personal letters to persons who do not trade with you, calling attention to your "Excellent lines" will bring you many a good and permanent customer. And if nothing results, no harm is done. Try it.

Sidewalk displays always work to good advantage. They pay well for the trouble consequent thereto, provided sufficient taste is displayed to attract attention. Nor is taste the only thing here, but attractive goods as well must figure, and plenty of them.

Keep well posted as to your business. Think not that your business will run itself. If you don't push your business your business will push you. Therefore keep posted that every advantage may be taken at the opportune moment of bargains that a slip shod dealer would through ignorance or negligence, let pass. I speak now generally and cover a large tract of ground, for unless you keep well posted, your better informed neighbor occupying more unpretentious quarters and carrying a smaller stock, will push to the front and show you his heels. Let me repeat, keep posted, and I know of no better vehicle of information than the incomparable RECORDER. Every issue is worth $20. Subscribe for it, preserve it, and keep it for reference.

When a man enters your store greet him as cordially as if he had entered your home. Grasp his hand, call him by name. Talk to him of things he is interested in. Ask him about his family, about "that sick horse," etc., and say a word for it. Your sale is more than half made. Prompt service cannot be over estimated.

Don't cut on prices, for you at the same time cut your own throat. Have a price and stick to it, and soon your customers will not expect a rebate, but they will too often insist upon it if you have a reputation for giving it. Insist always on a fit if possible. Fit the foot first, the head afterward. And I'm reasonably sure the good Lord will forgive us, if we slip a little French chalk in a No. 3 shoe that is about to receive a No. 5 foot.

In conclusion attend the National Convention and attend to your business.

How to Manage a Retail Shoe Store.

BY J. W. D. CHAMBERSBURG, PA.

With a desire to be helpful to others permit me to write a few points that I have found useful in the building up of a good paying trade in shoes. Having been a subscriber for the Recorder for only two months I am not familiar with the contents of the letters of the first series, except the last three or four, so if some of my points happen to be the same as those in former letters I will not be charged with plagiarism.

Of course, in a retail business, location comes first, and it is a very important point to be on the right side of the street. There is alway a best side, and I would pay one-third more rent to be on that side. For transient trade alone it will pay to make the difference.

Then make your store prominent. Money invested in good signs is always well spent. Make the store front so no one can walk by without knowing it is a shoe store and whose it is.

Arrange the store inside so that persons coming in will naturally feel at home and comfortable. Have a place where they can sit down, and always recognize them by a nod, a word of greeting, or a smile. Nothing is more natural than to feel hurt if you go into a store and stand for some time without being noticed.

A customer does not like to be hurried, and there are twenty ways of bringing a sale to a conclusion without seeming to be in a hurry. I have known splendid salesmen to seem to have lots of time when waiting on a customer yet be hurrying them right along. Never say "Will you take this pair?" or "Shall I wrap this pair up for you?" Help them to decide, but never ask them to. Better miss a sale than make one and have the customer go away dissatisfied with his or her purchase, and feeling that it was forced upon them, and make up their minds that they won't go there again.

Be patient and courteous and never lose temper. This does not mean to be servile, or to "grin and bear" every thing an unreasonable customer may say.

Keep the store neat and clean; it can be too neat, but never too clean. By too neat I mean the bad impression that is made upon a customer on entering a store where everything has a "Sunday appearance," as though nothing was going on. "Nothing succeeds like success," and nothing is better than to have customers feel that they have come to a store where crowds buy and business is brisk.

Keep the stock as much in departments as possible, using single cartons, and have the size, width and description marked plainly on the label. A very good plan is to use different colored labels for different sizes and styles, so that in putting away goods, especially after a rush, you can find the boxes quickly, and get them in their places. If a carton is put in the wrong place it is noticed at once, because that color of label does not correspond with those around it. It is an easy way to classify goods.

To keep heavy boots there is nothing better than a section of shelving fitted up with pigeon holes, each holding a pair of boots, and each row representing a size ; in this way each kind of boots will be right before you and you can put your hand right on the size called for without disturbing anything else. This plan once tried will never be abandoned.

Rubbers ought to be arranged in the same way. The pigeon holes should be large enough to hold half a dozen pairs of one size, and should be kept sized up. By this plan you never get your rubber stock tossed up.

Keep the show windows clean and well-lighted, and change the display in them frequently, so that people passing will expect to be paid for stopping to look in, and may be influenced by something they see to come in ; then, if treated rightly, you can secure a customer.

Liberal, judicious advertising always pays in the retail trade. It is very much like taking medicine ; if you don't take enough it will only make you sick, and do no good. Find the best medium and use it freely, but never allow an advertisement to get stale or promise more than you can perform. Keep it constantly before the public, and use every inducement to draw people to the store.

The cash system is by far the most pleasant way of doing business, besides the only safe way. The credit system will drive many a good customer away, because they don't like to face you while in your debt ; therefore, they take their cash to another store.

The dishonest man considers himself just so much ahead when given credit, and will talk against you and find fault with your goods to others to have an excuse for leaving you and buying elsewhere, when the real excuse is he owes you and don't want nor intend to pay you, so avoids you. In my humble opinion, corn meal and creek water is better for cash down than a whole barrel of flour bought on tick.

Keep posted on the markets and know whatever is to be known about the goods you handle. Keep thoroughly posted ! Use the knowledge thus gained in buying, and you will be recognized as an intelligent buyer, and there will be little danger of you paying too much for goods. The more you know about the trade the more pleasure you will have in the business and the more satisfaction you will experience in trying to manage a retail shoe store.

How to Manage a Retail Shoe Store.

BY M. E. KREIDLER, SOUTH BETHLEHEM, PA.

Experience, although oftentimes a dear teacher, is in reality the only true road to success. Therefore, in order to write an essay on "How to Manage a Retail Shoe Store," experience is very essential. If engaged or about entering business, we should possess the following qualifications, viz : knowledge of the goods, enterprise, energy, economy, perseverance, promptness, decision, foresight, affability, knowledge of human nature, and good memory of details. Capital and choice of locality, last but not least, must have some consideration. The better a man is acquainted with the details of the business in which he is engaged, the greater is his chance of success. Ignorance may occasionally win, yet the risk is too great to try. In purchasing shoes for retail purposes it is highly necessary to have a practical knowledge of what is required to make good, reliable and substantial shoes, and also to know fully the wants of your customers. It pays to insist on having and buying good, honest, all-leather goods. Innersoles, counters and shanks are very often overlooked and considered as a secondary matter, and of very little account whether solid or shoddy. Very often retailers find all at once that their sales are falling off, which, at the time, cannot be accounted for. Of course there are many other ways through which this will and may happen, yet the shoddy part in a shoe acts the quickest. In buying a shoe, say to retail at $1.25, $1.00 would, in the majority of cases, be the price paid in order to make the proper amount of average ; still, at said price you may not be able to secure all the leather and wearing qualities expected. Therefore, it is policy to pay five cents per pair more and get good counters, outer and innersoles. This rule should be followed in buying and selecting your entire stock.

Energy is natural to the healthy human body in most cases, yet it is the second requisite to even moderate success. Enterprise is the principal factor of a business qualification. It is not so essential in making merely a comfortable living, but of vital importance to any one who starts out with a desire to count his profits by the thousands. True enterprise takes note of everything which points to success, makes prudent calculations, and pushes ahead determined to win, and seldom allows rash ventures. "Economy is wealth." A careful avoidance of unnecessary waste and unneedful expenses in conducting a business, is of great value to a retailer. Accumulation must increase little by little ; want of attention in saving these littles, and looking after the petty details of the business will permit the profits to go as fast as made. "Be careful of the pennies and the dollars will care for themselves," is an old maxim, nevertheless a true one.

Open and unpack goods carefully; save the empty boxes and find sale for them. Nails likewise come handy if saved. Avoid cutting of string in opening packages; also any heavy paper not soiled serves very well when wanted. By keeping a record of these savings, you will, at the end of the year, have cause for surprise at former extravagance. On the other hand, do not allow economy to lead you to stinginess; be liberal and generous where business demands. Never use a newspaper or any soiled paper in which to wrap goods; it is the worst advertisement to have out. For heavy or rough shoes it may do, still it should be the exception not the rule. Have neatly printed wrapping paper different sizes; it will more than repay for the outlay.

Perseverance is necessary in almost any undertaking in life. A business is not built up in a year, often not in four or five years. The want of this trait of character is often visible in the affairs of those around us; some start in business and work faithfully for a year or more, but become wearied by the slow progress they are making, sell out their business, when possibly they are just on the eve of success. "Never say die." Try to increase sales from month to month and year to year. Making a customer is not so very difficult, but to retain after making is wherein the secret lies. Promptness and decision go hand in hand. You want plenty of push and snap; do not allow yourself to be driven by circumstances. Be wide awake and up with the times, carefully studying how to replenish your stock from time to time with new and fresh goods, and buy a limited quantity of any new styles offered (with which you should be familiar) enabling you oftentimes to dispose of some articles not so staple. Do not understand from this to buy every shoe called for. It would be an impossibility to satisfy all these imaginary wants without overstocking. Decision is here necessary ; decide at once whether the shoe offered will suit the trade and section. Still it is better to lose sometimes than never to make.

Copy or file all orders, and keep a record or memoranda of all orders given, stating terms distinctly, undersigned by the agent to whom the order is given (manufacturers or jobbers are held responsible for the acts of their agents). Aside from this it will give a complete idea as to the amount of goods sold and needed. Foresight comes to relief here and aids in calculating how trade is likely to be the coming season, which is of great importance to every retailer. To have an article when at its greatest demand, and steering clear of same before the demand ceases, comes from ability to see from present circumstances what the future is likely to require, and directing action by this probability.

Affability aids to retain customers when once made. Have a cheerful look and word for every one. It costs nothing but shows good results. See to it that clerks in your employ possess this excellent quality of worth. Ill manners, rude speech and deception in the sale of goods are the best traits imaginable to drive away trade. Knowledge of human nature enables any one to know when to speak, how to speak, and when to keep silent. Moderate flattery at the right time, as to the size or beauty of a lady's foot (gentlemen are not so particular) will oftentimes effect a sale which otherwise could not be made. Show a willingness to show the different kinds of shoes carried in stock, and at the same time try and ascertain the kind and price wanted.

It is best not to show the high-priced ones first. There are a great many shoes which every retailer keeps which he cannot expect to offer at less price than his competitors. Much depends on the ability to express ideas and suggestions politely; generally the buyer will purchase wherever he is most honestly, honorably and agreeably dealt with; especially does this hold good with cash customers.

A good memory to remember the faces and names of customers is very important. Address them by name, especially those who do not visit your place of business often; it creates a welcome feeling and aids in making sales. Retain prices paid for the different lines and grades of shoes so that you can feel satisfied that the stock has been well bought, which is advocated to mean half sold, still more so if combined with the qualities and arts as above stated.

Capital should be ample, just how much it is hard to say; it greatly depends on the locality, trade and competition. If a stock is, say $5,000, there should at least be a reserve of $1,000 to fall back on when needed, and so on, according as the stock and trade increases, Ready cash is one of the best friends in

business. Pay as you go is a very good motto, and
should be more universally adopted. The good pay-
ers are generally sought after, and get the benefit of
low prices.

Discount all bills if it can possibly be done. If
business is done on the cash down system (which is
by far the most preferable and least expensive way)
the problem as to capital is not such a difficult one.
Quick sales, turning stock often is the way to make
the most money, and to do business with a smaller
amount of capital, which does not alone consist of
the ready cash put in business. A good name with
an established credit must also be considered as part
capital, as the one is nearly as often used as the
other. To do business with money alone and no credit,
would be found very inconvenient or perplexing.

Location should be the best that can be secured,
however, in keeping with the amount of capital invested. Rent should not be high merely to secure
the location desired; sales should warrant the high
rent. Location on a street out of the line of business
travel, or too far up or too far down on a street will
often prove very disadvantageous. Trade is found in
stores centrally and conveniently located. There is,
therefore, a great advantage in having a location so
convenient to the buyers that when going out to make
purchases they first come there. Special care should
be taken to make the store look attractive, clean and
inviting. A place for everything and everything in
its place. Windows, show cases and floors should
show signs of cleanliness. Patrons will observe these

points very quickly, especially ladies. Have all the modern improvements in the way of tools and machinery, thus saving much time and labor, and rendering the waiting on customers much easier. Examination, marking and arranging of goods must not be overlooked. After goods are received in store, unpack, carefully examine every pair (if shoes) to see if damaged. Note that they come up to the sample shown. If errors or damages are discovered report them at once to the manufacturer or wholesale dealer. After examination of every article, or pair of shoes, they should be plainly marked with cost and selling price. Small paste labels are very convenient, and the shank of the shoe is the proper place for them as they do not rub off very easily; still they can be removed if so desired, which is the case sometimes where the price is not to be known, or when wanted to use as a present. Much depends on the neatness and appearance shown in the marking of shoes. Clearness of the mark is very essential. It looks very unbusiness-like to see a salesman or proprietor when waiting on a customer turning an exhibited article in order to search for the mark, all the while allowing your customer to wait. The marked cost should not only be prime cost of invoice, but should include the expense of purchase, freight and charges up to the time the goods are delivered into the dealer's place of business, especially so where goods are bought at net prices. The true cost being ascertained, the next consideration will be the profit to be made, which is not a very easy problem to solve, and no special rule can be given. Some goods command a better profit than others, and it is well to notice the different proportions that will probably be sold of each kind. Shoes in which fashion or style makes a large part of the value, and which a change of fashion will make less valuable, must bear a higher percentage than staple or every day sellers. The expense account must, to a certain extent, be your guide in regulating profits. An excellent way to notice whether profits are sufficient is to make an occasional day's record of your sales, together with the kind, quantity and price, with the cost on the margin.

Arranging of goods is a study in itself, but if properly done will have a pleasing and attractive effect. Plenty of light, and so arranged as to show the goods to the best advantage, is very necessary. Keep shoes in cartons as much as possible. Have them arranged in departments: ladies', misses', gents' and boys', and let convenience be the motto in every department. In keeping rubbers it is well to have enough of each size, keeping the different sizes and kinds separate, and the balance of duplicate stock should be kept in a dry, cool place, as a cellar, if dry.

Advertising we should never forget. How, when, where, and to what extent are important points which need close study. One thing is necessary, that is to keep the name and place of business prominently before the public. Home papers are very good mediums in which to advertise. Cards, pencil tablets and blotting pads for school use with dealer's name secures the good will of the children, which is, in most cases, the most difficult thing to obtain ; and every dealer should be aware of the importance of this. Selling honest goods at fair prices, and polite, courteous treatment, are as previously stated, never to be forgotten.

Guard against losses by fire, theft, neglect, and various other ways. Be master of your business and guard it with a jealous care. Keep fully insured. Pay your clerks fair and living wages, giving them no cause for any dishonest transactions.

Old or shop-worn boots or shoes should never be allowed to accumulate. Changes of cost at the end of each year, or some mark placed on shoes when bought, will show you, by going over stock, which are staple and which stale or shelf goods.

A rubber stamp (with dealer's name, place of business and changeable date) to stamp all shoes on the lining, will be found a most excellent way by which many a dispute can and may be settled. Dealers generally have the same troubles to contend with, namely : claims for wearing qualities of shoes. Who has not heard remarks like the following, or similar ones : "These shoes were bought of you just three weeks ago, never wore them more than once or twice ; they are of no account, ripped, and counters all crooked." You look in the inside of the shoes for the date stamped therein, which is now almost invisible, and that alone will prove the falseness of your customer's statement. Further examination will disclose that instead of three weeks' wear three months have elapsed since they were purchased.

Where the stamp mark is gone, your customer has no just claim, and should be treated politely ; still a long argument is unnecessary.

Have your own brands of shoes made for you. Buy of manufacturers as much as possible. Have neat and tasty signs throughout the store with names of the different brands carried in stock. Make attractive window and pavement displays, changed according to the season ; during rainy or snowy weather have all rubber goods displayed ; during fair weather the fancy wares. It is always an advantage when a dealer is considered by the community as having the leading store in the place. This can be accomplished by hard and earnest work. The lead once secured, the road to success lies plain before us.

How to Manage a Retail Shoe Store.

BY "HIC JACET".

In your conditions for essays on "How to Manage
a Retail Shoe Store, you do not limit the style in
which they are to be written, and I therefore take the
liberty of giving you a sketch of my business career
in my own way, which may suit your columns.

I was born in Skeneateles, Ohio, of poor, but honest parentage. [They always are—ED.] My father and
all his collateral relations had always paid 100 cents
on the dollar (sometimes more). I had a plain common school education, went into mercantile life at
the age of fourteen, and was twenty-two when I was
married to a most estimable young lady, still my wife.
Divorces don't run in our family. In my selection
of a help-meet I had followed Ben Franklin's advice,
to take one of a family of girls, for he reasoned that
they would be apt to improve each other, not copy-
ing each others' failings. Very true for Ben. Your
readers must put up with a great deal of irrelevant
matter, in order to understand my drift. The panic
of '73 wound up the concern where I had been working, at the munificent salary of $15 a week. By
economy I had saved about $1,800 at that time, and
having a good knowledge, as I thought, of the retail

shoe business, I sailed in. I had plenty of breadth
of beam and staying qualities. I opened a store 20x
60, double show windows on a good street, and
bought most of my stock for cash in small lots, and
of standard make. I was attentive, worked hard, had
small expenses and made no money. Could do no
more than pay as I'd go, etc. At a family council
held at my home on New Year's, or just after taking
account of stock, my mother-in-law—by the way I
had forgotten to mention I had married a daughter
of said mother-in-law, and she was a most important
factor in this article—my mother-in-law, as I said
before, in her mild, moral and methodical way, said,
"John, dear, what is the trouble, you don't seem to
make any headway. If I had thought you would be
able to do no better for my pet Jennie (all her daugh-
ters were her pets), you should never have had her.
Why look at Joe, Bill, etc., (my brothers-in-law,)
every one of them has failed, and all are well fixed
now. Why don't you fail, and then retire?" My
dear reader, did you ever have a note meeting, or did
you ever walk out to meet a note? If you did, you
can understand the fevered chill that ran up my back,
and down my spine at that suggestion. I fail? Never!
I'd be sold out by the sheriff first.

But a woman's tongue is never done. I had no
peace at home or abroad. I made up my mind to
fail, come what will. But how? I must increase my
stock, sell the stuff, pocket the money, and allow my
creditors to indulge in whistling for their cash. I did
it. I commenced to buy longer lines and got them,

distributed handbills, advertised special bargains, and commenced sacrificing, yes, slaughtering goods. What was the result? Crowds of people found that John Doe's place was the spot where big bargains are got. I doubled my business, I had considerate neighbors, too, who did me the favor of predicting to their trade that I would fail in a little while. They told people that some of the goods they were buying would never be paid for, and of course the public were anxious to get some of the loot. Nine out of ten retailers that read this article will claim and rightfully, that I was especially favored by fortune in my unholy ambition, to fail by their very neighborly comments on my ultimate fate, and I was; for three stores in my neighborhood, which at the time each did three times the business of my store, made no effort to counteract my methods any further than to announce by placards "We give full value," "We pay 100 cents on the dollar and give it." "There is no such word as fail," "No sheriff here." And I on the contrary was drumming into the ears of the public "At half price," "Given away," Your last chance," Only thirty days longer," and such chestnuts. But it took. I will show to anyone desirous of details, that I got better prices for nine-tenths of my goods than I ever dreamed of getting. At the same time I cut my credit by claiming, "No profit in the business, must have cash." I also made a masterstroke in announcing in the "Daily Trumpeter" that I would take no more scrip. There were a number of large factories in that town, that issued such to their hands, and I don't believe that $100 worth had been offered in my store in payment of goods in five years. These poor people working in these factories had always patronized a few stores especially favored in this way, and my declination to accept scrip or orders made my stock a sort of forbidden fruit, and they would have it. Besides the heads of these factories made a bitter fight on me, and that made it doubly interesting. My place was too small presently, and a larger store being idle two squares below, I rented it at three times the rent I had been paying, fitting it up regardless of expense, —for was I not going to fail, and my creditors would have it all to pay? It was the most attractive place in town in any line ; handsome settees, lounges, tete-a-tetes, (especially adapted to young couples,) mirrors, handsome salesmen (leaders of the german every one), salesladies, nice quiet Sunday School damsels, errand boys in full uniform, etc. I made my place the sensation and the centre of the town. The Court House and Theatre were side shows.

In order to establish relations with different jobbers and manufacturers, I was exceptionally affable to drummers, they made my store their first objective point. Inquirers from agencies were answered as suited my purpose (not too rose colored). It did not require that, the store was jammed constantly, and a look of go-ahead-ativeness pervaded everything. In fact money kept pouring in so constantly, that I got in the habit of discounting my bills, a very poor habit you will say, in order to fail. Not altogether. What I was after was a good line of credit, and I got it. I kept putting in stock, lines that my competitors did not dare to keep, and they took.

I became wofully extravagant in advertising, for I reasoned that when the time came, I should be able to explain where the money went. I took an entire column in the different papers published in the county. Had a wagon traveling all over the roads and crossroads of the neighborhood with odds and ends, to sell the farmers right out of it. Of course not one in ten could get what they wanted, and came to the store after it. The bell on this rig alone, cost me $40, but it woke up the country round about, although it did not wake up the competitors, for they all knew "such mountebankism won't go down with the public long." "Wouldn't last another six months anyhow." A circus had its baby elephant, oppose the progress of the 19th century in the shape of a gravel train, and at the cost of $250, this elephant did duty in front of my store, and thus wound up an inglorious career by getting into the shoe business. I gave prizes for athletic exhibitions and exposed them in my window. I started a base ball nine and equipped it, gave a purse for trotting match at county fair, in short in every way *I kept my name before the public*. I got as much gratuitious advertising almost as I paid for. But that isn't managing a retail shoe store, is it, dear reader? But I tell you it is. Well, dash it, I didn't fail. My attempt at failing was a failure. The old Irishman's proverb "Better to have bad luck than no luck at all," seemed to fit me. I did not succeed in failing, but I did succeed in building up the finest retail trade in the vicinity, and have got it still. I felt compelled to disappoint my mother-in-law and all the croakers in town, who were sure I'd bust. But I haven't given in yet. I am pegging away, giving away goods all the time, and making a better profit than any of my competitors. I started in to humbug my creditors, but only succeeded humbugging the public, and that is the great secret of success. It may not sound moral nor practical, but I have done it ; and so can you, or anyone else. Promise something for nothing, or next to nothing, and give it and you gain not alone a customer, but an advertiser. Try it, you will be convinced. Rush in a little bankrupt sale once in a while. Don't get rusty, keep moving. I would go into details regarding my methods of advertising, but consider it good policy to give the RECORDER a chance to start a new series on "How to advertise," and I will give my experience.

How to Manage a Retail Shoe Store.

BY M. A. R., ELK RAPIDS.

The store should be in as good a location as circumstances allow, wide as possible and long enough to divide into as many departments as the business requires, with plain fixtures extending well up, shelves movable and ledge wide enough to answer for counters. Draws should be narrow and deep, all grained in oak, or oil finish. (they being less liable to show marks from soiled hands). Shelf boxes should be labeled, white or colored. A good style of settee is double width with low back through the centre. Those made of all wood with perforated seats are cleaner and more comfortable in warm weather. Heavy mats of the same length are better than long strips of carpet and easier cleaned. A good assortment of tools and a large block to use them on will save a good many dollars in enabling you to do considerable small repairing.

Make a good display of samples in the store and windows. I advocate price cards on all medium and cheap goods, and some popular names on fine grades. I find a large proportion of customers like to inspect ·samples and learn prices without having to ask salesmen. In fact every means should be taken to make patrons feel at home, and that they can depend on what is told them in respect to material and service,

Stock should be bought with great care and arranged as regards kinds and sizes in the way most convenient to handle. Study the wants of the trade and endeavor to meet it without overloading. Buy of as few houses as possible, and after your lines are established keep them well sized·up. It is best to have goods coming in fresh often. Then, too, you are enabled to take advantage of the market in every way, and are not worried with an overstock which must be closed out at cost or less.

When you find a shoe fits and wears well, stick to it and give the maker to understand that you will as long as such is the case. It is far better in the long run to pay a little more for just what suits your trade than get something at a less price which fails to give entire satisfaction. I think all goods should have either the makers' or dealers' name stamped on them. It is a good guarantee to the buyer, and one of the best and cheapest means of advertising. The old chestnut that goods well bought are half sold is never too old to apply in the shoe business.

If your stock is purchased mostly of agents it will pay to go into the market at least once a year. A great many new ideas can be picked up and you will be able to keep up with the times, which is very necessary as business is done nowadays.

Clerks should be of medium size with good health and spirits, so that they will have a good stock of patience, and also be able to endure the severe strain

which during busy times is very trying. It is very
necessary that they understand the anatomy of the
feet in order to fit properly. They should also learn
enough of human nature to know when to fit the head
or feet or both. Handling the feet is a very delicate
matter, and salesmen cannot be too careful. In all
cases possible customers should be prevailed upon to
be fitted in the store. You then have an opportunity
of seeing where the shoe pinches and suggesting a
remedy. A customer will be more apt to rely on the
salesman in all future purchases. Patrons are often
annoyed by having the size and looks of their feet re-
marked upon both in and out of the store. Such a
practice will drive away those who otherwise might be
valuable. Above all, salesmen never should fail to
study the wants of the buyer and if possible endeavor
to furnish what is the most suitable in style, fit and
service. Never deceive in mentioning the stock, and
always be ready to exchange when there is the least
dissatisfaction. Sit in front of your customer when
fitting ; for that purpose two seats are necessary, a
high one for yourself and a lower one for the customer's feet.

Advertising is a very important factor and should
be studied as a part of the business. Every means
should be used to let the public know your's is the
place to get comfort for their feet. Newspapers and
other special ways are desirable, but the most sure
way is to treat your patrons in such a manner that they
consider your shoes are ahead of all others. My way
of doing it is to explain what a good fit it is and have

them satisfied. When such is the case their shoes will give better service and be worn with a good deal more comfort. To bring it about requires patience and a thorough insight into the business.